Comfort

Comfort

Edited by

Christopher Howse

continuum
NEW YORK • LONDON

CONTINUUM

The Tower Building, 11 York Road, London SE1 7NX

15 East 26th Street, New York, NY 10010

www.continuumbooks.com

First published 2004

British Library Cataloguing-in-Publication Data
A catalogue record for this book is available from the British Library.

ISBN 0-8264-7297-4

Typeset by Aarontype Limited, Easton, Bristol
Printed and bound by MPG Books Ltd, Bodmin, Cornwall

Contents

Introduction

The world is so full of a number of things – one must agree with Stevenson – I'm sure we should all be as happy as kings. In the sunshine, the heart leaps up whenever it sees a rainbow in the sky, a daffodil beside the lake or a baa-lamb in the field. Human beings are designed to enjoy themselves, to be happy.

It is pleasurable even to look at natural surroundings. The celebration of natural beauty neither began nor ended with the Lake Poets.

> So many lovely things, and if a man looks on them,
> And his mood is not softened, nor a smile on his face,
> An intractable clod is he, at odds with his heart is he,

wrote Marbod of Rennes in the 11th century. And such is the effect of beauty on the observer that it is hard not to think that the world reflects the glories of its creator. In the late 19th century Gerard Manley Hopkins wrote a sonnet making the connection explicit:

> The world is charged with the grandeur of God.
> It will flame out, like shining from shook foil.

The apparent order and intricacy of nature moved even the empirical scientists who have come to dominate the world of learning since the 17th century. In London, Nehemiah Grew (1641–1712), a leading figure in the newly founded Royal Society, made important discoveries in plant anatomy (establishing, for example, the sexual reproduction of flowering plants). What is more, the regularity and beauty of inanimate substances filled him with awe. In his microscopic observation of ice formation he noted:

> Sometimes a Company of Little Icy Globules, that is, Misly
> Drops which have been suddenly frozen by the Snow, will be
> so piled one upon another as to compose a Little Pyramid
> terminating in one single Globule at the Top, not much
> unlike to a Lavender Spike. And sometimes several flat Ici-
> cles will be so composed as to resemble a Mallow Flower.

Grew devoted a large book (*Cosmologia Sacra*, 1701) to showing the
evidences for the designing hand of God in the world and its
history. But in reading it, one cannot help thinking that he was as
fully impressed by a sense of the numinous, the godly wonder, of
the world.

Two centuries later, another man with well developed powers
of observation, Francis Kilvert, returned again and again in his diaries to the beauty of the Wye valley on the Welsh borders where
he lived. Here he says the scene at 11am on a November morning
was 'indescribable' in its loveliness, but he makes a good attempt at
describing it:

> The wet village roads shone like silver below, and the market
> folk thronged past the Vicarage and School. A railway
> engine sent up a bright white jet of steam over the bank
> from Hay Station, the oaks were still tawny green and glit-
> tering with diamond dews, Hay Church in a tender haze
> beyond the gleaming of the broad river reach and rapids
> above the Steeple pool. How indescribable, that lovely bril-
> liant variegated scene. A rook shot up out of the valley and
> towered above the silver mist into the bright blue sky over
> the golden oaks, rising against the dark blue mountains still
> patched and ribbed with snow.

There is a sort of satisfaction too in the regular homely events of a
peaceful life. There is a flavour of this in the diaries of another clergyman, a hundred years before Kilvert, James Woodforde. His
engaging habit of recording what he had for dinner has given some

an impression that he was a gourmand. In reality his diet was the common one of the 18th-century gentleman, and a fairly plain one. There was beef or mutton, often boiled, and fish when the weather was not too hot; there were fowl and game if someone gave a bird as a gift; there were green peas to enjoy when they came into season and there was an invariable batter pudding or plumb pudding (as he spelled it); there was always wine or beer. But life was more active; Woodforde was always going about his parish on horse or on foot. It froze in the bedroom in winter. More calories were consumed than by a sedentary desk-worker today. In any case, it is not the scale of the consumption that comes over in the diary decade by decade, so much as the common round of the days, weeks and seasons. Year by year Woodforde christens, marries and buries his parishioners; his servants give trouble or satisfaction; he has his tenants to dinner; his niece shows hopeful signs of finding a husband. Human life is there, and it is good.

Dinner is delicious today, and tomorrow dinner time will come again. Dinner implies a dinner table, with friends, a spouse, children. There is love and marriage and friendship. We take our pleasures socially. If we enjoy beauty in nature we enjoy it too in art made by another person. We share the pursuit of the beautiful and the good, of the good life, with people we know or people whose thoughts we read. We stand on the shoulders of past giants. The progress of civilization makes things more beautiful, more developed, easier, more comfortable.

This enjoyment of the world can go beyond enjoying this or that particular thing in it, and there can appear an amazed intuition of the fact that things exist. That fact is itself an engine of delight. This sort of existential discovery was made after a period of dark pessimism during his art-school years by G.K. Chesterton. He came as a young man to hold a rough sort of theory:

> Even mere existence, reduced to its most primary limits, was extraordinary enough to be exciting. Anything was magnificent as compared with nothing. Even if the very daylight

were a dream, it was a day-dream; it was not a nightmare. The mere fact that one could wave one's arms and legs about (or those dubious external objects in the landscape which were called one's arms and legs) showed that it had not the mere paralysis of a nightmare. Or if it was a nightmare, it was an enjoyable nightmare. In fact, I had wandered to a position not very far from the phrase of my Puritan grandfather, when he said that he would thank God for his creation if he were a lost soul.

Why then compile a book called *Comfort*, if everything is already so good? Isn't comfort something that a mother gives to a child that has grazed a knee? Yes, it is, and it is more than our knees that are grazed. If toothache makes dinner uneatable we go to a dentist. To whom should we go for heartache?

Fundamentally, I am convinced, everything is going to be all right. 'All shall be well, and all shall be well, and all manner of things shall be well,' as Julian of Norwich heard Jesus say to her. It was not taken trivially by her. But in the meantime it is not all daffodils and baa-lambs. People we love die. We all die. Things hurt us. People do bad things. We do bad things, even when we hardly mean to. And then we are left in a horrible confused state of not liking to be told about 'sin' but not seeing how to get rid of feeling bad about human behaviour, our own included.

If fundamentally everything is going to be all right, it is not because everything is all right now. We need to realize how bad the state of affairs is if we are to know how good the news is that it can be mended. I do not intend to be pessimistic. On the contrary, the plain object of this book is comfort. Nor is it necessary to drink the dregs of the world's sorrow and horrors. There is enough to be going on with in our ordinary lives.

What kind of comforts do we hope to find? The history of the word comfort itself suggests some. As a verb the earliest meaning, from the 14th century is 'to strengthen (morally or spiritually)'; but the dictionary adds 'Obsolete'. Perhaps so, but there is a survival of the meaning in the Bible, especially in St Paul. In his second letter to the Corinthians he speaks of 'the God of all comfort, who comforteth us in all tribulation, that we may be able to comfort them which are in any trouble, by the comfort wherewith we ourselves are comforted of God'. That suggests a sort of strength, and a grace that gives power to spread itself. It also involves a meaning of the noun comfort, 'Relief or support in mental distress or affliction; consolation, solace soothing', to which the dictionary adds in parenthesis: 'In later use sometimes expressing little more than the production of mental satisfaction and restfulness'. Even so, there is a fundamental relief and support in the words of Isaiah, 'Comfort ye, comfort ye my people saith your God.' That verse in Latin has *consolamini*, and there is an overlap between comfort and consolation. Consolation reaches its feeblest sense in a 'consolation prize', and comfort in the notion of being comfortable, comfy, with an absence of pain. There is a fabric conditioner called Comfort, and this suggests that, even at its feeblest, being comfortable is something, like chocolate, that people will pay good money for.

When the poet P.J. Kavanagh published his excellent anthology *A Book of Consolations* in 1992 he made the point that a mere collection of things 'at first sight "cheering" would end up depressing us'. He quotes Francis Bacon's remark, 'Even in the Old Testament, if you listen to David's harp, you shall hear as many hearse-like airs as carols: and the pencil of the Holy Ghost hath laboured more in describing the afflictions of Job than the felicities of Solomon'.

The felicities of Solomon are likely to be far less comforting, too, than the story of Job. Paradoxically, it is necessary to face the seriousness of the situation in order to be in a position to receive the comfort that is there to be gathered. In a letter to a friend in 1939, in the middle of a period of inner anguish, which stretched on and off from 1932 to 1947 (although he did not know it was to come to an end), David Jones explained the argument of a book he was trying to write: 'I think it is really about how, if you start saying in a kind of way how bloody everything is, you end up in a kind of

xiii

praise – inevitably – I mean a sort of Balaam business. Yes perhaps it will be called *The Book of Balaam*, or *Book of Balaam's Ass*. A Spot of Job too!'

This is an insight shared by Katharine Mansfield. The journals of her fatal encounter with tuberculosis during the First World War are not free from the heightened emotions popularly associated with that disease. But one day, in considering something she had read about the apparently repellent role of creatures parasitic on human beings, she is suddenly struck by the rightness of everything altogether – notwithstanding her own unfulfilled desires for life.

> I had a sense of the larger breath, of the mysterious lives within lives, and the Egyptian parasite beginning its new cycle of being in a water-snail affected me like a great work of art. No, that's not what I mean. It made me feel how perfect the world is, with its worms and hooks and ova, how incredibly perfect. There is the sky and the sea and the shape of a lily, and there is all this other as well. The balance how perfect. I would not have the one without the other.

This is 'a kind of praise,' in David Jones's words.

Yet since the happy ending is not immediate, we need in the meantime to possess courage and a trust in providence, which is to say that everything will one day be all right. Courage comes in because sorrow is very tiring. The mind keeps coming back to the thing that is giving trouble, like the tongue to an aching tooth, and this is boring. Courage at least makes it possible to face adversity even when no happy ending is in sight. This is true in war, when the enemy may be winning, and it is true in pain or bereavement when there seems no cure. With the sorrows of everyday life, it is seldom possible to run away; the sorrows come too. (But, then, it is not at all easy to run away in war.) Yet, the fantasy of running away has its appeal all the same. Courage is the faculty that enables us to carry on despite the remembrance that this is another day without an answer. Sometimes the courage is so deep within the heart (the central core of the person), that its presence is only discernible after the events have passed. It is the kernel of integrity that in after years allows us to say: 'It was terrible at the time, and I still feel it, but I would not want it to have been otherwise.'

If the heart is to have any hope, then it must hold on to providence. If there is no providence, then human beings are in a fundamentally tragic position in the world. By providence I mean the care that God gives to those who keep his commands. He has promised them justice and beatitude as a correlative of the commands he enjoins. I do not say that if we break our relations with God everything is lost, for he is always faithful, and he never does break his own promises, and his promises entail an undertaking to have mercy and forgive the sinner who repents – which is everyone. At the same time, the guarantees of providence show that we cannot hope to benefit by betraying our friends or our country, by lying or stealing or harming others. Indeed the only safety is in keeping the compact with God. It might lead to death (though it often works out that it is the only way – the unforeseen way even – to avoid death). But death itself has by faithfulness been converted from tragedy into the birth of happiness.

The nub of the tragic quandary of human beings is that everyone wants to be united with God in some way, to go to heaven, but has, since the Fall, been incapable of achieving that destiny – 'conscious, however dimly, of the desire to please God, yet with no apparatus for doing it', as Ronald Knox put it. Augustine of Hippo had seen the same thing 1500 years earlier: for a really happy life, there must be the prospect of immortality. 'No one is wrong to want immortality if human nature is capable of receiving it as God's gift,' he wrote. 'If it is not capable of it, then it is not capable of happiness either.'

Oddly enough it was the liberal, half-believing Spanish intellectual Unamuno, who put the difficulty most sharply. For him, the defining characteristic of the sense of the tragic is an unquenchable thirst for immortality. 'I want to be my self, and without ceasing to be my self to be all others as well, to penetrate into all things visible and invisible, to extend myself into limitless space and to prolong myself into time without end. If I am not all and for ever, it is as if I were nothing,' he wrote in *The Tragic Sense of Life in Men and Peoples*. This far he could go, but Unamuno was never to resolve his confused apprehension of the role of reason in external religion, or to reconcile his reverence for inherited culture with the demands of modernity and democracy.

If, however, the genre of tragic myth is applied to the drama of the life of Jesus, it emerges as a very peculiar tragedy. First of all, in the life of Jesus, the tragic flaw that classically leads to a disastrous ending is not a vice, such as family pride, jealousy, impiety or hubris. Jesus dies on the cross because he is unwilling to exert the power that the tempter in the desert had already invited from him – to summon a legion of angels or rule the whole world. He is made like sinful humanity as far as his weakness goes, but he has committed no sin that deserves that debility. (When Julian of Norwich writes of sin she often means the painful consequences of sin both for Jesus and for us who follow him.) Yet, it is suggested, by exhibiting a flaw that is no vice but mere humility and weakness, Jesus is made greater than any other power. By voluntarily embracing death he destroys it, and by rising from the dead he triumphs over sin, and the suffering and offence it causes. Instead of a pagan catastrophe at the end of the drama, there is a 'eucatastrophe', a happy ending. Instead of the evils of a disturbed society bringing down the tragic hero, the hero heals the whole society of mankind – then and now – by triumphing over evil in his own person.

Another difference between classical dramatic tragedy and the story of Jesus is that dramatic tragedy is made up, and the story of Jesus is an historical fact. A fictional myth may be a way of expressing human insight into a tragic circumstance, and from that shared insight deriving some consolation. But St Paul very reasonably observed that if Christ did not rise 'we are of all men most miserable'. If the claims of Christianity are not true then we are back in the old tragic impasse. If they are true, then all history is redeemed, and the story of every life acquires a meaning.

For all that, the happy ending is still not reached for each of us. I have placed two accounts of a journey at the beginning of this book because each person is a *viator*, a journeyer. If he knows he is a pilgrim to the city of peace, as Walter Hilton says, still the road is long, uncertain and hard, with the dangers of robber, bad weather, thirst and tiredness. Every pilgrim has trouble keeping up his own spirits, in staying on the road, and in retaining confidence that it is the right road to a real place.

We meet many along the way with contradictory notions. There are, for example, opportunities for human beings to kid themselves about their true standing in the world. Some make themselves the heroes of a dream played out for their own entertainment. They see themselves as Prometheus or Loki, the tragic rebel hero, even if their own tragedy has been brought on by their own moral shortcomings – cowardice, betrayal, cruelty, self-harm. This *ignis fatuus* of egotistical defiance is exemplified in mundane lives by those fearful favourites of *Desert Island Discs*: 'My Way' and 'I Will Survive'. The choice of these anthems not only indicates a psychologically flawed self-image, as the hero or heroine of all that occurs within the universe, but also, I suspect, invites widespread ridicule of those who choose them.

Yet there is room for bragging in the face of inimical forces, and such defiance can be poetically powerful. 'I am the master of my fate/ I am the captain of my soul,' wrote W.E. Henley in his 'Invictus' – although neither statement was true. It was pitiful that Timothy McVeigh, the man convicted for the Oklahoma bombing in 1995 which killed 168, should choose that short poem as his 'final written statement' before execution.

I am unsure whether Emily Brontë's poem 'No Coward Soul Is Mine' might not fall in this category. The poem is sometimes used as a hymn. I know that she invokes 'God within my breast', but is this 'life – that in me has rest, as I – undying Life – have power in Thee' really God? Perhaps it is. The poem certainly has been read as if it is, and thus it has power to strengthen and console.

In a similar way, John Donne's 'Batter my heart, three person'd God' is a defiant boast. Not that the poet is on the surface challenging God. The images he uses are violence and sexual conquest, and it seems that he is inviting God to act violently towards himself. It is as if he is defying his own bodily resistance to grace, and calling down upon himself scouring fire and blows and divine rape. Yet, is there a hint of the poet shouting at God, 'Come on then, do your worst'? The degree to which the narrator of the sonnet is sincere in his invitation, is an ambiguity consistent with Donne's art as a poet.

Another poem, which does not use the word God but surely refers to him, is Hilaire Belloc's 'The Winged Horse' (page 94). Belloc has, in general, suffered from his admirers and some of his own bombastic traits, but this poem, or song, successfully uses the convention of boasting to point up the narrator's almost tragic state of being. Even in reading its triumphalistic central section on the heavenly armies of Christendom, it is worth remembering that the hero Roland died fighting against overwhelming odds for his king. The poignancy comes from the first and last sections, with their images of the flint-cut homeless feet of the bereaved, and the concluding claim to a 'spouting well of joy within that never yet was dried'. A recording exists of Belloc as a very old man singing this song in his reedy voice. Belloc, as Ronald Knox pointed out tellingly, surprises the reader with sublimity in the midst of light verse and with jokes in solemn passages. His 'Ballade of Illegal Ornament' starts out jauntily and ends with the moving: 'Jesus, in mine Agony, / Permit me, broken and defiled, / Through blurred and glazing eyes to see / A Female Figure with a Child.'

Song, no doubt of it, adds another dimension to poetry. Partly it summons up, like a familiar smell from long ago, the irresistible force of memory. But it works within its own métier too. Gavin Bryars' remarkable piece of 'found poetry' set to music consists entirely in the following words reiterated on a loop and accompanied by his own music: 'Jesus' blood never failed me yet. Never failed me yet. Jesus' blood never failed me yet. There's one thing I know, for he loves me so . . .'

As words on the page, they seem a commonplace scrap of an old hymn. Bryars has given his own account of how he came to appreciate the power of this fragment.

> In 1971, when I lived in London, I was working with a friend, Alan Power, on a film about people living rough in the area around Elephant and Castle and Waterloo Station. In the course of being filmed, some people broke into drunken song – sometimes bits of opera, sometimes sentimental ballads – and one, who in fact did not drink, sang a religious song 'Jesus' Blood Never Failed Me Yet'. This was not ultimately used in the film and I was given all the unused sections of tape, including this one . . .
>
> When I played it at home, I found that his singing was in tune with my piano, and I improvised a simple accompaniment. I noticed, too, that the first section of the song – 13 bars in length – formed an effective loop which repeated in a slightly unpredictable way. I took the tape loop to Leicester, where I was working in the Fine Art Department, and copied the loop onto a continuous reel of tape, thinking about perhaps adding an orchestrated accompaniment to this. The door of the recording room opened on to one of the large painting studios and I left the tape copying, with the door open, while I went to have a cup of coffee. When I came back I found the normally lively room unnaturally subdued. People were moving about much more slowly than usual and a few were sitting alone, quietly weeping.

Whatever pleasure people find in listening to Bryars' composition, they do not experience the raw pain of sorrow. Perhaps their feelings are analogous to those of audiences watching a stage tragedy. The experience may be cathartic, but not in the same way as the agonies supposed to be suffered by the characters on stage. Instead there is a comfortable sympathetic sorrow, a pleasurable fictional sorrow.

This kind of feeling might be genuinely fruitful for Christians who contemplate the sufferings, the Passion, of Jesus Christ, to whom they attribute their own salvation. Certainly it has been the business of painters from Grünewald to Rembrandt in their different ways to evoke emotion in the Christian who looks at their representations of a suffering Christ. So it was Bach's intention in his Passions. But people go to hear the *St John Passion* for pleasure, and non-believers go too. That does not mean that Christians, moved in their emotions by seeing or hearing, cannot then be moved in their deeper hearts to adjust their way of knowing and loving Jesus. It may start in their senses and emotions, but it is bound to, since how can anything new come into their minds except through their senses? Nevertheless, they should be aware that a comfortable feeling of sympathy, even a feeling of poetic anguish (as though for the fictional King Lear), is not the same thing as a change of heart towards the real person of Jesus.

The vital part which that truth has in our religious sentiment is nowhere more clearly apparent than in the unwelcome but insistent apprehension that we – I – have done things I ought not to have done. The vague sense of sin is only too prevalent in this decade or so of history. People feel like labradors that have made a muddy track on the best carpet; they feel guilty without quite knowing how they came to do anything that could summon up this feeling. And yet if guilt is to be conquered we must recognize true sin for what it is. It is hard to have the courage and honesty to recognize sin as an offence against reality and its creator. I should say that it can only be faced if we have the strengthening assurance that it is possible to be forgiven, truly forgiven, by the highest authority. The maker of all, including our selves as we are, can forgive and wash us and heal us.

THE COMFORT in this book is taken from Christian authors in the English-speaking tradition, or if not from writers in English, from writers such as Augustine of Hippo or Boethius, whose works have been adopted by a tradition of English-speakers. Otherwise I would have included material from the treasure-house of Orthodox devotion *The Philokalia*, say, or from Edith Stein, who, though named as a patron of Europe, is hardly yet familiar to an English-speaking public.

There is much comfort in writings outside the Christian tradition, in Plato and Virgil, in Philo and Maimonides. There is even beautiful poetry written by the late Ayatollah Khomeini. It is also the case that in the early centuries of Christianity a great debate about the admissibility of pagan thought was settled by the integration into Christian culture of the bits of pre-Christian thought that were deemed true. 'Greek philosophy does not comprehend the whole extent of the truth,' wrote Clement of Alexandria around the beginning of the third century. 'Besides, it is destitute of strength to perform the commandments of the Lord. Yet, it prepares the way for the truly royal teaching.' A pagan world-view has just as much need – I would argue much more need – for comfort, but in this book I want to draw specifically on the Christian resolution of the tragic postulate.

Self-imposed rules of exclusion also mean I have kept out biblical passages, though the books of Job, the Song of Solomon, Jonah, are full of comfort, and the whole of the Psalms. Here at least I have allowed in an example or two of the psalms that have been pulled from the Bible to become the solid core of congregational worship and private prayer – Psalm 19, on the stars, and Psalm 38, a prayer of forgiveness. There is much in the versions of the Psalms in the *Prayer Book* translation of Coverdale or the liturgical Latin version that is extra-biblical in the strict sense. They share, for example, some of the elements of a school song, a nursery rhyme, a favourite poem, a prayer learnt by heart, a phrase that comes to mind unbidden. They are familiar, not like the multiplication tables but like the rooms of a childhood home; they are transferred like a map on to the soul and help it find its way.

I should like to have included more poetry by John Clare, Gerard Manley Hopkins, Robert Herrick, George Herbert; more extracts from John Bunyan, Augustine of Hippo, John Donne. The works of these writers are easy to find if you want more. I could have taken two dozen stories from the extraordinary collection made by John Spencer, the librarian of Sion College in the mid 17th century, and his book is hard to get hold of. All these writers had their troubles and their flaws, but each holds tight to something worth keeping.

To quote P.J. Kavanagh again, 'There is consolation in good writing', and I have certainly found much in the passages chosen. The poetry is more or less designed to catch the susceptibilities of the soul, but plain prose at its best is as good as a walk over open moorland. That is the prose of Ronald Knox, for example. Newman's is a bit more worked up. The cadences of John Donne are sublime, and the incremental nibbling at his text that Lancelot Andrewes practised is something that no writer now would attempt, though in the language of the early 17th century it has a great power of penetration.

From the spring flowers of Prudentius in the fourth century to the contemporary concerns of Harry Williams or Ruth Burrows, this collection represents a constant appetite among thinking, feeling people down the ages. We want happiness and shall never rest and be comforted till we find it.

I was putting together this book while my mother was dying. Now she is dead. If the passages chosen here are put to the test, do they comfort me? Not in the way that I might be comforted by an aspirin if I had a headache, no. But mourning has different stages, and they can start before the bereavement. As it happens, some of the thoughts of the writers here have helped. There is more to it, though, than the consolations of poetry or the timeliness of an apposite observation. In the end it is fruitless to seek comfort in literature or art. Only in the Spirit that on occasion can be discerned behind them is to be found a comfort that the world cannot give.

Life's journey

A very pleasant day
Francis Kilvert

Francis Kilvert (1840–79) left charming diaries of his life as a country clergy-man on the Welsh marches in the 1870s. He excelled in describing the beauties of nature. He was also sensitive to the attractions of women, and at last happily married in August 1879, only weeks before dying unexpectedly of peritonitis.

Wednesday, 15 April 1874   A bright hot sun and cold east wind, the sky a deep and wonderful blue and the roads dry. Teddy and I decided to go up today to Overton on the Marlborough Downs. We went by train to Calne at ten o'clock.

The little town looked bright, busy and happy in the morning sunshine, one boy carrying a bundle of white osiers and another standing on a green mount playing a concertina. A glance into the noble church with its Norman pillars and arches but the worshippers were kneeling and the deep solemn tones of the priest's voice came down from the Choir. It was the time of morning prayer and as we had not time to remain and join in the service we closed the door reverently and came away.

In the presence of the great silent White Horse on the hillside at Cherhill, we turned into the Black Horse for some ale. Then on and on over the long white road stretching up and down but rising ever across the backs of the great rolling downs, with the sun glaring hot and scorching on our right hand, and the NE wind piercing keen on our left.

Soon we came in sight of the first outlying barrow rising over a shoulder of the down – solemn, mysterious, holding its secret in unbroken silence and impenetrable mystery. There was a ceaseless singing of larks in the vast empty expanse of the sky and down. They

1

were rising in the sunshine all over the hills. The monotony of the downs was broken here and there by spinneys and scattered lonely clumps of trees, chiefly fir and beech. Teams of horses and oxen were crawling slowly along the great slopes at plough and harrow, and one team of four white oxen harrowing in the distance seemed scarcely to move at all. The grey tower of Yatesbury Church rose among the grove of trees which sheltered the village, far on the left. The keen wind hummed a melancholy song among the telegraph wires and each post had its own peculiar measure and mournful song. Solitary barrows rose here and there upon the heaving down.

The sun glared blinding upon the white flint road and the white chalk land, and the great yellow dandelions by the road side stared at the sun. On, on, up the interminable road winding like a white ribbon over the green downs till at length we climbed to 'Needle Point', the highest ridge, and began to descend towards Beckhampton. As we got between hedges, once more the banks were snowy with black thorn blossom and the country was filled with the bleating of flocks.

Then the King of the Barrows, strange, vast, mysterious Silbury Hill came in sight, the great problem, the world's puzzle, with the white chalk landslip on its steep lofty green slope. . . .

At Kennet, our eyes were refreshed by the vivid green of the rich low water meadows and the soft murmur of the streams, and our hearts by the thought of the strong Kennet ale that we should get at Overton.

Along the crest of the last ascent, Seven Barrow Hill, the five remaining barrows rose in a line marking perhaps the graves of an army that had been destroyed in defending the road.

As we descended the hill towards Overton and the little wayside Bell Inn came in sight, a sad presentiment seemed to come over my brother that the kind people, the Hamlins, who were so kind to him when he stayed at the inn with a sprained foot last harvest, were dead or gone away. The old name, Sarah Hamlin, was still over the door. A young man was lounging in front of the house. 'Is Mrs Hamlin at home?'

2

'Mrs Hamlin,' repeated the young man mechanically. 'Mrs Hamlin's dead.'

He was her son. My brother was much distressed. It was a great and sudden shock. 'Miss Hamlin's at home,' added the young man. Sophie Hamlin came into the little parlour, a tall beautiful girl in deep mourning with a sweet firm small mouth and singularly brilliant dark eyes. 'Do you remember me?', said my brother sadly. She knew him at once. The little wayside inn round which bright happy memories clustered, had become a sorrowful place. Her mother died suddenly a month ago.

After luncheon I walked back alone along the hot glaring white road to Beckhampton, leaving my brother and sweet Sophie Hamlin to talk together for awhile, for they were old friends. He followed me after a while.

I found Mr Pinniger oiling his mowing machine on his return from the Board of Guardians at Marlborough. He gave us tea and showed us the line of the old Roman road from Calne to Marlborough and London. The road avoids Silbury Hill and makes a detour round it, showing that the hill is older than the road. This fact has been proved by excavation. In harvest time, the line of this Roman road may be distinctly traced, for the wheat growing along the line of the road is ripe some days earlier than anywhere else on the down.

We got to Calne just in time to catch the 6.50 train to Chippenham after a very pleasant day.

Lift me o'er the stiles
Robert Herrick

Robert Herrick (1591–1674), though a clergyman, is generally thought of as a poet celebrating the attractions of women. But he applied the same facility for turning light-seeming verses to sacred subjects in Noble Numbers *(1648) from which the poem below is taken.*

To his ever-loving God

Can I not come to Thee, my God, for these
So very-many-meeting hindrances,
That slack my pace, but yet not make me stay?
Who slowly goes, rids (in the end) his way.
Cleere Thou my paths, or shorten Thou my miles,
Remove the barrs, or lift me o'er the stiles:
Since rough the way is, help me when I call,
And take me up; or els prevent the fall.
I kenn my home; and it affords some ease,
To see far off the smoaking Villages.
Fain would I rest; yet covet not to die,
For feare of future-biting penurie:
No, no, (my God) Thou know'st my wishes be
To leave this life, not loving it, but Thee.

The vision of peace
Walter Hilton

Walter Hilton (who died in 1396) was one of a number of great English mystics who flourished during the 14th century. He lived as an Augustinian friar. His book The Ladder of Perfection, *was printed 100 years after his death by Wynkyn de Worde, a collaborator of Caxton's. His analogy of the Christian life on earth with that of the pilgrim, was taken up by Augustine Baker, the 17th-century compiler of the best spiritual advice. Just as the destination, Jerusalem, has the meaning of a place of peace, so our own peace, he says, is found in Jesus.*

SINCE you desire to know some way by which you can come nearer to reform in feeling; with the help of God I will tell you what seems to me to be the shortest and easiest way, and I will do so by taking the example of a pilgrim.

A man wished to go to Jerusalem and, because he did not know the way there, he asked another man who, he hoped, would be able to tell him. This man replied that he would not be able to get there without great difficulty and labour, for the way, he said, is long and dangerous because of thieves and robbers, and there are many obstacles in the way of a man going there. Furthermore, there are several roads that seem to lead to it, but every day men are slain and robbed and cannot reach their destination.

There was however, he said, one road by which he would guarantee that a man should reach the city of Jerusalem, and not lose his life on the way. He would be robbed and beaten and suffer great distress, but his life would be saved. Then the pilgrim said, 'As long as my life is spared and I come to the place I desire, I do not mind how much I have to suffer on the way. Whatever advice you give to me I will promise to carry it out.'

The other man replied, 'Well, I will set you on the way. This is it, and you must carry out the instructions that I give you. Do not stop over anything that you hear, or see, or feel that would hinder you on your way. Make no pause for it, do not look at it, do not take pleasure in it, do not fear it. Keep on your way and have no aim but to be at Jerusalem, for that is what you desire and nothing but that. And if you are robbed, or beaten, or treated with contempt, do not resist, if you wish to keep your life. Put up with the harm you suffer and continue as though nothing had happened, lest you should suffer greater harm. And if men wish to keep you by telling you false tales to amuse you and turn you from your pilgrimage, do not listen and do not reply to them, but only say that you wish to be at Jerusalem. And if men offer you gifts and to make you rich with this world's goods, pay no heed to them, keep your mind always on Jerusalem. If you will keep to this way and do as I have said, I will answer for it that you will not be slain but that you will come to the place that you desire.'

In the spiritual sense Jerusalem is the vision of peace and represents contemplation in the perfect love of God. For contemplation is nothing else than the vision of Jesus, who is true peace. And if you desire to come to this blessed vision of true peace and to be a pilgrim to Jerusalem, I will put you on the way as far as I am able, even though I have never been there myself.

The beginning of the way is reform in faith, and this, as I have said, is based on humility and faith and the laws of the Church. You can be assured that whatever sins you may have committed before, if you have been reformed by the sacrament of Penance according to the law of the Church, you are in the right way.

Now if you wish to make good progress, there are two things that you must often have in mind, humility and charity. That is, I am nothing, I have nothing, I desire only one thing. The sense of these words must be your constant guide, even though the words themselves are not formulated in your mind, for that is not necessary.

Humility says, I am nothing, I have nothing. Charity says, I desire only one thing; and that is Jesus.

These two strings united by the thought of Jesus will produce harmony in the harp of your soul, when they are skilfully touched with the finger of reason. The lower you strike on one, the higher the other will sound. The less you feel that you are, or that you possess, through humility, the more you will desire to possess Jesus in love. I am not referring to the humility that a soul feels at the sight of its own sin or weakness and at the misery of this life, nor yet that which it feels at the sight of the virtues of other men, for though such humility is genuine and helpful, still it is harsh and worldly, not pure, and gentle, and charming.

But I am referring to humility that the soul feels through grace in the contemplation of the infinite being and the great goodness of Jesus. If you cannot yet see this with the eyes of your spirit, believe that it is so. For the knowledge of his being that comes through perfect faith or through contemplation will make you consider yourself not only the most miserable creature in existence, but as absolutely nothing, even though you had never committed a sin. And such humility is beautiful.

For in comparison with Jesus, who is in truth all, you are nothing. And in the same way you ought to judge that you possess nothing, but are like an empty vessel that has no power to fill itself. For however many exterior and interior good works you perform, till you are conscious of the love of Jesus, you have nothing. For with that precious liquor only, may your soul be filled and with no other. For since that alone is so precious, consider anything that you have and do as unable to satisfy you without the contemplation and the love of Jesus. Put everything else behind you and forget it that you may have that which is best.

A real pilgrim going to Jerusalem leaves house and lands, wife and children, and strips himself of all his possessions that he may go easily on his way without hindrance. In the same way, if you wish to be a spiritual pilgrim, you must strip yourself of all your possessions; good works as well as bad, you must put them all behind you, and make yourself so poor in spirit that you rest in no work of your own, but are always desiring the grace of greater love and are always seeking the spiritual presence of Jesus. If you do this then you are setting your heart wholly on being at Jerusalem and nowhere else but there. Your heart is wholly intent on having nothing but the love of Jesus and what spiritual vision of himself he will give you.

It is for that alone that you were created and redeemed; that is your beginning and your end, your joy and your happiness. And therefore, whatever you possess, that is, however rich you may be in good works, hold it as nothing as long as you have not experienced this love of which I am speaking. If you keep this purpose before you and cling to it earnestly, it will bring you safe through the perils of your journey. Thieves and robbers may despoil and beat you, that is the evil spirits may attack you with various temptations, but your life will always be spared. In a word, if you will follow my instructions, you will escape all dangers and quickly come to the city of Jerusalem.

To be a Pilgrim
John Bunyan

John Bunyan (1628–88) wrote this set of verses to go with The Pilgrim's Progress *(1678), though they are better known in an adaptation for congregational singing made by Percy Dearmer (1867–1936).*

Who would true valour see,
Let him come hither;
One here will constant be,
Come wind, come weather.
There's no discouragement
Shall make him once relent
His first avowed intent
To be a pilgrim.

Whoso beset him round
With dismal stories
Do but themselves confound;
His strength the more is.
No lion can him fright,
He'll with a giant fight,
He will have a right
To be a pilgrim.

Hobgoblin nor foul fiend
Can daunt his spirit,
He knows he at the end
Shall life inherit.
Then fancies fly away,
He'll fear not what men say,
He'll labour night and day
To be a pilgrim

A wonderful world

The secret fire
William Cowper

William Cowper (1731–1800) found himself so overcome by depression that he had to give up his profession as a lawyer. He lived in quiet retirement in Huntingdon with Morley Unwin and his wife Mary, and, after Mr Unwin's death, at Olney, Buckinghamshire, with Mary Unwin and her family. Who knows but if his melancholia might have responded better to the active regular life of a seafarer, perhaps, as had once been followed by his friend the Revd John Newton (author of 'Amazing Grace'). Instead he made the best of an unexciting daily round by writing poetry and pleasantly composed letters to his friends. From 1785 he composed a much admired long poem 'The Task', deliberately reserving for the latter parts explicit consideration of the work of God in nature. The passage here comes from the sixth book, The Winter Walk at Noon.

What prodigies can pow'r divine perform
More grand than it produces year by year,
And all in sight of inattentive man?
Familiar with th' effect we slight the cause,
And, in the constancy of nature's course,
The regular return of genial months,
And renovation of a faded world,
See nought to wonder at. Should God again,
As once in Gibeon, interrupt the race
Of the undeviating and punctual sun,
How would the world admire! but speaks it less
An agency divine, to make him know
His moment when to sink and when to rise,
Age after age, than to arrest his course?
All we behold is miracle; but, seen

So duly, all is miracle in vain.
Where now the vital energy that mov'd,
While summer was, the pure and subtile lymph
Through th' imperceptible meand'ring veins
Of leaf and flow'r? It sleeps; and th' icy touch
Of unprolific winter has impress'd
A cold stagnation on th' intestine tide.
But let the months go round, a few short months,
And all shall be restor'd. These naked shoots,
Barren as lances, among which the wind
Makes wintry music, sighing as it goes,
Shall put their graceful foliage on again,
And, more aspiring, and with ampler spread,
Shall boast new charms, and more than they have lost.
Then, each in its peculiar honours clad,
Shall publish, even to the distant eye,
Its family and tribe. Laburnum, rich
In streaming gold; syringa, iv'ry pure;
The scentless and the scented rose; this red
And of an humbler growth, the other tall,
And throwing up into the darkest gloom
Of neighb'ring cypress, or more sable yew,
Her silver globes, light as the foamy surf
That the wind severs from the broken wave;
The lilac, various in array, now white,
Now sanguine, and her beauteous head now set
With purple spikes pyramidal, as if,
Studious of ornament, yet unresolv'd
Which hue she most approv'd, she chose them all;
Copious of flow'rs the woodbine, pale and wan,
But well compensating her sickly looks
With never-cloying odours, early and late;
Hypericum, all bloom, so thick a swarm
Of flow'rs, like flies clothing her slender rods,
That scarce a leaf appears; mezerion, too,

Though leafless, well attir'd, and thick beset
With blushing wreaths, investing ev'ry spray;
Althaea with the purple eye; the broom,
Yellow and bright, as bullion unalloy'd,
Her blossoms; and, luxuriant above all,
The jasmine, throwing wide her elegant sweets,
The deep dark green of whose unvarnish'd leaf
Makes more conspicuous, and illumines more
The bright profusion of her scatter'd stars.
These have been, and these shall be in their day;
And all this uniform, uncolour'd scene,
Shall be dismantled of its fleecy load,
And flush into variety again.
From dearth to plenty, and from death to life,
Is Nature's progress when she lectures man
In heav'nly truth; evincing, as she makes
The grand transition, that there lives and works
A soul in all things, and that soul is God.
The beauties of the wilderness are his,
That make so gay the solitary place
Where no eye sees them. And the fairer forms
That cultivation glories in, are his.
He sets the bright procession on its way,
And marshals all the order of the year;
He marks the bounds which winter may not pass,
And blunts his pointed fury; in its case,
Russet and rude, folds up the tender germ,
Uninjur'd, with inimitable art;
And, ere one flow'ry season fades and dies,
Designs the blooming wonders of the next.
Some say that, in the origin of things,
When all Creation started into birth,
The infant elements receiv'd a law,
From which they swerve not since. That under force
Of that controling ordinance they move,

And need not his immediate hand, who first
Prescrib'd their course, to regulate it now.
Thus dream they, and contrive to save a God
Th' incumbrance of his own concerns, and spare
The great Artificer of all that moves
The stress of a continual act, the pain
Of unremitted vigilance and care,
As too laborious and severe a task.
So man, the moth, is not afraid, it seems,
To span omnipotence, and measure might
That knows no measure, by the scanty rule
And standard of his own, that is today
And is not ere to-morrow's sun go down!
But how should matter occupy a charge
Dull as it is, and satisfy a law
So vast in its demands, unless impell'd
To ceaseless service by a ceaseless force,
And under pressure of some conscious cause?
The Lord of all, himself through all diffus'd,
Sustains, and is the life of all that lives.
Nature is but a name for an effect,
Whose cause is God. He feeds the secret fire
By which the mighty process is maintain'd,
Who sleeps not, is not weary; in whose sight
Slow circling ages are as transient days;
Whose work is without labour; whose designs
No flaw deforms, no difficulty thwarts;
And whose beneficence no charge exhausts.
Him blind antiquity profan'd, not serv'd,
With self-taught rites, and under various names,
Female and male, Pomona, Pales, Pan,
And Flora, and Vertumnus; peopling earth
With tutelary goddesses and gods
That were not; and commending, as they would,
To each some province, garden, field, or grove,

But all are under one. One spirit – His
Who wore the platted thorns with bleeding brows –
Rules universal nature. Not a flow'r
But shows some touch, in freckle, streak, or stain,
Of his unrivall'd pencil. He inspires
Their balmy odours, and imparts their hues,
And bathes their eyes with nectar, and includes,
In grains as countless as the seaside sands,
The forms with which he sprinkles all the earth.
Happy who walks with him! whom what he finds
Of flavour or of scent in fruit or flow'r,
Or what he views of beautiful or grand
In nature, from the broad majestic oak
To the green blade that twinkles in the sun,
Promote with remembrance of a present God!

The threshold of Spring
Christina Rossetti

*Christina Rossetti (1830–94) wrote the remarkably uncomfortable quatrain,
'Does the road wind uphill all the way? / Yes, to the very end. / Will the day's
journey take the whole long day? / From morn to night my friend.' Still, later in
the poem, there are 'beds for all who come' in the inn at the road's end.*

*Other of her poems reflect the rich colouring of the Pre-Raphaelite world she
inhabited. 'A birthday' ends: 'Raise me a dais of silk and down; / Hang it with
vair and purple dyes; / Carve it in doves and pomegranates, / And peacocks with
a hundred eyes; / Work it in gold and silver grapes, / In leaves and silver fleurs-
de-lys; / Because the birthday of my life / Is come, my love is come to me.'*

More neglected today are her prose works on religious themes. In Seek and
Find *(1879) she methodically contemplates the Benedicite, a canticle from the
Book of Common Prayer that takes the text of the song of the three holy children
in the fiery furnace, found in the Septuagint version of the Book of Daniel. Since
the boys were in the midst of the fire, their praise of both fire and heat, summer
and winter, are the more impressive: 'O ye Fire and Heat, bless ye the Lord:*

praise him and magnify him for ever. O ye Winter and Summer, bless ye the Lord: praise him and magnify him for ever. O ye Dews and Frosts, bless ye the Lord: praise him and magnify him for ever.' The following passage is Christina Rossetti's notes on the word 'Winter and Summer'.

'Lo, the winter is past' (Song of Solomon, 2:11)
'The summer is ended.' (Jeremiah, 8:20).

Winter and summer are unlike at a thousand points. Winter has bareness, cold, the aspects and circumstances which produce and result from these: Summer has exuberance, heat, and all their delightful train. In one thing they are alike both 'pass,' both 'end.' Their likeness is absolute, their unlikeness is a matter of degree merely. For the bareness of Winter is yet not without many a leaf, and its coldness is warmed and brightened by many a sunbeam: the exuberance of Summer brings not forth the treasures of other seasons, nor does its heat preclude the blast of chilly winds. Both pass, both end.

Winter by comparison lifeless, leads up to Spring, the birthday of visible nature: Summer, instinct with vitality, ripens to the harvest and decay of Autumn. Winter at its bitterest will pass: Summer at its sweetest must end. It is emphatically 'while the earth remaineth' that Summer and Winter shall not cease (Genesis, 8:22): in the better world which is to come we find no trace of either; nor of cold, and expressly nor of heat (Revelation, 7:16); and though leaves and fruit appear (22:2), no mention is made of flowers, so characteristic of the Summer we love.

Just because we love it and revel in it, Summer is steeped for us in sadness: at the longest its days shorten, at the fairest its flowers fade, next after Summer comes Autumn, and Autumn means decay. Winter, even while we shrink from it, abounds in hope; or ever its short days are at the coldest they lengthen and wax more sunny. Winter is the threshold of Spring, and Spring resuscitates and reawakens the world. Winter which nips can also brace: Summer which fosters may also enervate. There is a time for all things (Ecclesiastes, 3:1), all things are double against each other (Ecclesiasticus, 42:24), and God hath made all things good (Genesis, 1:31), for all are his servants (Psalm 119:91).

The seasons of the waxing and waning year have an obvious parallel in the periods of our mortal life; a parallel so obvious that it need not be drawn out in detail, for to speak of one series is to describe the other. Also, the privilege and, so to say, the duty of both are the same: 'All are His servants.'

Pyramids like lavender
Nehemiah Grew

Nehemiah Grew (1641–1712) was a leading member of the Royal Society and was in the forefront of scientific discovery. His speciality was plant anatomy, and he made good use of new microscopic techniques, observing, for example, the reproductive functions of flowering plants. His Cosmologia Sacra *(1701) ranges over the whole scientific world and the contents of the Bible, demonstrating the nature of God from his effects. Grew argues for the omnipotence of God from the marvellous design of creation, and he is not embarrassed to see creatures as extremely convenient for mankind. The cosmos was a friendly place. But implicit in his argument is a sense of wonder, amounting to the numinous, in the beautiful regularity that new scientific observations were constantly uncovering.*

It hath been observed by others that in Snow there are many Parts curiously Figured, commonly into little Starry Icicles of Six Points. But in a Discourse presented to the Royal Society, and published in the Philosophical Transactions, I have demonstrated that the whole Body of a Snowy Cloud consisteth of such and other-like Icicles regularly Figured. That is, that the very Small Drops of a Misling Rain, descending through a Freezing Air, do each of them shoot into one of those Figured Icicles. Which Icicles, being ruffed with the Wind in their Fall, are most of them broken and clustered together into small Parcels which we call Flakes of Snow.

The Agency of the same Freezing Principle is also very fine here below. In a Hoar-Frost, that which we call a Rime is a Multitude of Quadrangular Prismes, exactly Figured, but piled without any Order, one over another. In the first Frost upon a Snow I have seen the like Prismes so piled one upon another and joined End to End, and equally encreased in their Length, as to compose a Sexangular and Inverted Pyramid, somewhat like the Bowl of a Funnel. And sometimes a Company of Little Icy Globules, that is, Misly Drops which have been suddenly frozen by the Snow, will be so piled one upon another as to compose a Little Pyramid terminating in one single Globule at the Top, not much unlike to a Lavender Spike. And sometimes several flat Icicles will be so composed as to resemble a Mallow Flower.

The Dew upon Windows and Water upon flat, smooth and broad Stones will sometimes be elegantly flourished into a Vegetable Form. The Congealing Principle being assisted herein by the Volatile Parts of Plants, which continually perspire, and hover in this Lower Region of the Air in greater Plenty.

In a freezing Season, if a Glass-Plate or a Window-Square be made all over wet with warm Water, that it may not freeze too suddenly, it will, upon Freezing, always shoot regularly: one Parcel of Striae running Parallel, being Obliquely and always at the same Angles intersected by another Parcel, viz: the same Angles as there would be in Snow if the several Icicles thereof consisted only of a Pair of Striae.

Whereby it is plain that not only in all the former Examples but wheresoever Water is divided into smaller Parcels, or lies in a very thin Body in proportion to its Surface so as the Congealing Principle hath Power enough to command it, and the freezing Striae have room enough to shoot forth and are not over-numerous so as to be confounded, it will still be regularly Figured. . . .

Now Regularity, which is certain, cannot depend upon Chance, which is Uncertain. For that were to make Uncertainty the Cause of Certainty. Suppose we then, that any Figures may be made by Motion upon Matter. Yet Regular Figures can never come but from Motion Regulated, and therefore not Casually made. For then it would be Casually Regular, or by Rule by Chance, which is Nonsense. It is therefore evident that, as Matter and Motion, so the Cizes and Figures of the Parts of Matter have their Original from a Divine Regulator. The curious and manifold Varieties of which, could we see, they would doubtless make as fine a show as all the Beauties of Nature which lye before us. . . .

Of that great Variety we have of Minerals, Animals, and Plants, how few are Noxious compared with those which are Friendly to us? And in every Species of those which are the most Useful we have the greatest Plenty.

A great many Plants will hardly with Nursing be made to live, much less to thrive and to produce their Seed, out of their Native Soil and Country. But Corn, so necessary for all People, is fitted to grow and to seed as a free Denison all over the World.

Among Animals, a Sheep, for the same Reason, feeds and breeds in all Countries much alike. And those which are Domestick or more Useful are also more Prolifick than the Noxious or less Useful of the same kind: as Hens are than Kites; Geese than Swans; Coneys than Hares; Dogs than Foxes; and Cats than Lyons. A Crane, which is scurvy Meat, lays and hatches but two Eggs in a Year. And the Alka, and divers other Sea-Fowls, lay but one. But the Pheasant and Partridge, both Excellent Meat and come more within our reach, lay and hatch Fifteen or Twenty together. And those of Value which lay fewer at a time sit the oftener, as the Woodcock and the Dove.

And what is more admirable than the Fitness of every Creature for the Use we make of him? The Docility of an Elephant, anciently much employed in War; the Insitiency of a Camel for travelling in the Deserts of Africa and other Parts; the Gentleness of a Sheep in the field and when she comes to the Slaughter. A Horse is swift and strong above most other Animals, and yet strangely Obedient. Both Comely and Clean, he breeds no sort of Vermin; his Breath, Foam and Excrements, Sweat, Urine and Dung are all sweet. Fitted every way for Service or Pleasure, the meanest, or the greatest Matter. And as for those Beasts which are Armed and Fierce, they are so made not with Intent to hurt us, but to defend themselves or seize the Prey, which they also usually seek in the Night, when men are retired from their Business and safe at home.

No intractable clod
Marbod

Marbod of Rennes (1035–1123) is not very widely read in the Anglo-Saxon world since most of his work remains untranslated from Latin. But some of his poetry was rendered into English by Helen Waddell (1889–1965) who brilliantly introduced the modern reader to the world of medieval poetry. Marbod led a lively youth but quietened down after becoming a bishop. At the age of 88 he resigned his diocese and withdrew to the Benedictine monastery of St Aubin at Angers, his place of birth.

Now must I mend my manners
And lay my gruffness by.
The earth is making merry,
And so, I think, must I.
The flowers are out in thousands,
Each in a different dress.
The woods are green and like to fruit,
The earth has donned her grassy fleece,
And blackbirds, jackdaws, magpies, nightingales
Shouting each other down in equal praise.

There's a nest in the tree with young ones in it,
And lurking in the branches are the unfledged birds.
The bearded grain is whitening to harvest,
Lovely are the gardens with the half-blown rose;
Add to these the vines, and the grapes, and the hazel nuts.
The young girls dancing, and their mothers dancing too,
And the young men at play, and the good feast toward.
And the quiet shining day.

So many lovely things, and if a man looks on them,
And his mood is not softened, nor a smile on his face,
An intractable clod is he, at odds with his heart is he,
For he who can behold earth's beauty without praising it
Has a grudge against earth's Maker, whose honour all
    these serve,
Cold winter, summer, autumn, comely spring.

Glad that I live
Lizette Woodworth Reese

Lizette Woodworth Reese (1856–1935) was a schoolteacher in Baltimore for 45 years who began publishing poetry in 1874.

A Little Song of Life

Glad that I live am I;
That the sky is blue;
Glad for the country lanes,
And the fall of dew.

After the sun the rain;
After the rain the sun;
This is the way of life,
Till the work be done.

All that we need to do,
Be we low or high,
Is to see that we grow
Nearer the sky.

Like an Aethiop bride
William Habington

William Habington (1605–54) made his name with a volume of poems Castara, *mostly addressed to his wife, in the mannered style of the reign of Charles I. The stanzas here are from his poem 'Nox nocti indicat scientiam', a quotation from Psalm 19 (according to the numbering in the King James version; Psalm 18 in the Vulgate).*

When I survay the bright
Coelestiall spheare,
So rich with jewels hung, that night
Doth like an Aethiop bride appeare,

My soule her wings doth spread
And heaven-ward flies,
Th' Almighty's mysteries to read
In the large volumes of the skies.

For the bright firmament
Shootes forth no flame
So silent, but is eloquent
In speaking the Creator's name.

No unregarded star
Contracts its light
Into so small a Charactar,
Remov'd far from our humane sight:

But if we stedfast looke,
We shall discerne
In it as in some holy booke,
How man may heavenly knowledge learne.

The bridal chamber
Augustine

Augustine of Hippo (354–430) took a verse of Psalm 19 'the bridegroom, goes forth from his bridal chamber', which is literally a similitude of the sun in the sky. But in his sermon (No 291, on the Birthday of John the Baptist, preached in one of the years 412–416), he applies it to Jesus, the Word of God, wedding himself to the flesh of mankind in the bridal chamber of the womb of the Virgin Mary. It is a 'metaphysical' conceit that William Habington would have admired. In a tour de force of close meditation, Augustine the great preacher hammers home the pure gift of grace by which the Incarnation of Jesus is achieved.

What art you, Mary, who will presently give birth? How have you merited this, whence have you obtained this favour? Whence is it that he who made you will be made in you? Whence, I say, does this great gift come to you? You are a virgin, you are holy, you have vowed a vow. True, you have merited much, or better, you have received much. But how have you merited it? He who made you is being made in you. He by whom you yourself were made is made in you; rather should I say, by whom heaven and earth were made, by whom all things were made. The Word of God is made flesh in you by taking flesh, not by losing divinity.

The Word is joined to flesh; the Word is wedded to flesh, and the bridal chamber of this exalted marriage is your womb. Let me repeat, the bridal chamber of this exalted marriage between the Word and flesh is thy womb, whence 'he, the bridegroom, goes forth from his bridal chamber' (Psalm 18:5). He finds you a virgin at his conception. He leaves you a virgin at his birth. He brings you fruitfulness. He does not take away your integrity. From where does this come to you?

Perhaps I am too forward in asking such questions of a virgin and, I might say, somewhat rude in shocking your modest ears with such words. But I see a virgin who is indeed bashful, and yet one who can answer and at the same time put me in my place.

21

'Are you asking me from where this comes? I blush to answer your questions as to my blessedness. Rather, listen to the Angel's salutation. Believe him whom I believed. Are you asking from where I receive this favour? Let the Angel reply.'

Tell me, Angel, from where has Mary received this?

'I have already said when I saluted her: 'Hail, full of grace.''

Half for the eagle
Bede

Bede (673–735), as well as being an admirably reliable historian, had a sensitivity to nature that he learnt in part from the tradition of his spiritual master St Cuthbert. His Life of Cuthbert *(721) is full of sympathetic respect for God's creatures.*

It happened, that on a certain day he was going forth from the monastery to preach, with one attendant only, and when they became tired with walking, though a great part of their journey still lay before them before they could reach the village to which they were going, Cuthbert said to his follower, 'Where shall we stop to take refreshment? Or do you know anyone on the road to whom we may turn in?'

'I was myself thinking on the same subject,' said the boy, 'for we have brought no provisions with us, and I know no one on the road who will entertain us, and we have a long journey still before us, which we cannot well accomplish without eating.'

The man of God replied, 'My son, learn to have faith, and trust in God, who will never allow those who trust in him to perish with hunger.' Then looking up, and seeing an eagle flying in the air, he said, 'Do you perceive that eagle yonder? It is possible for God to feed us even by means of that eagle.'

As they were talking, they came near a river, and saw the eagle standing on its bank. 'Look,' said the man of God, 'there is our good servant, the eagle I spoke to you about. Run, and see what provision God has sent us, and come again and tell me.'

The boy ran and found a good-sized fish, which the eagle had just caught.

But the man of God reproved him, 'What have you done, my son! Why have you not given part to God's servant? Cut the fish in two pieces, and give her one, as her service well deserves.'

The dearest freshness
Gerard Manley Hopkins

Gerard Manley Hopkins (1844–89) observed nature closely, recorded it in his notebooks and compressed it in his poetry. He took to himself the idea of Ignatius Loyola, the founder of the Society of Jesus, that the goodness of God is clearly discernible in creation. Claiming the support of the theologian Duns Scotus, Hopkins saw even in inanimate nature a sort of individualistic and existential declaration of God's glory.

God's Grandeur

    The world is charged with the grandeur of God.
    It will flame out, like shining from shook foil;
    It gathers to a greatness, like the ooze of oil
    Crushed. Why do men then now not reck his rod?
    Generations have trod, have trod, have trod;
    And all is seared with trade; bleared, smeared with toil;
    And wears man's smudge and shares man's smell: the soil
    Is bare now, nor can foot feel, being shod.

    And for all this, nature is never spent;
    There lives the dearest freshness deep down things;
    And though the last lights off the black West went
    Oh, morning, at the brown brink eastward, springs –
    Because the Holy Ghost over the bent
    World broods with warm breast and with ah! bright wings.

At home

Indoors, soft and dry
Robert Herrick

*Robert Herrick (1591–1674) appears in the character of a simple-living coun-
tryman in this poetic exercise from* Noble Numbers *(1648).*

Thanksgiving to God, for his House

Lord, Thou hast given me a cell
Wherein to dwell
A little house, whose humble Roof
Is weather-proof;
Under the sparres of which I lie
Both soft, and drie;
Where Thou my chamber for to ward
Hast set a Guard
Of harmless thoughts, to watch and keep
Me, while I sleep.
Low is my porch, as is my Fate,
Both void of state;
And yet the threshold of my doore
Is worn by th' poore,
Who thither come, and freely get
Good words, or meat:
Like as my Parlour, so my Hall
And Kitchin's small:
A little Butterie and therein
A little Byn,
Which keeps my little loafe of Bread
Unchipt, unflead:
Some brittle sticks of Thorne or Briar

Make me a fire,
Close by whose living coale I sit,
And glow like it.
Lord, I confesse too, when I dine,
The Pulse is Thine,
And all those other Bits, that bee
There plac'd by Thee;
The Worts, the Purslain, and the Messe
Of Water-cresse,
Which of Thy kindnesse Thou hast sent;
And my content
Makes those, and my beloved Beet,
To be more sweet.
'Tis Thou that crown'st my glittering Hearth
With guiltlesse mirth;
And giv'st me Wassaile Bowles to drink,
Spic'd to the brink.
Lord, 'tis thy plenty-dropping hand,
That soiles my land;
And giv'st me, for my Bushell sowne,
Twice ten for one:
Thou mak'st my teeming Hen to lay
Her egg each day:
Besides my healthfull Ewes to beare
Me twins each yeare:
The while the conduits of my Kine
Run Creame (for Wine).
All these, and better Thou dost send
Me, to this end,
That I should render, for my part,
A thankfull heart;
Which, fir'd with incense, I resigne,
As wholly Thine;
But the acceptance, that must be,
My Christ, by Thee.

Happy in your house
Alcuin

Alcuin (735–804) went as a boy to the cathedral school at York, of which, aged 43, he became the head. He was renowned for his learning and ability in building up a library and body of teachers. In 782 he went to Aachen to organize the renaissance in learning envisaged by Charlemagne. Fourteen successful years later he retired from the palace school to become abbot of St Martin's monastery, Tours, living another eight years. The Latin quatrain below was translated by Helen Waddell.

When you sit happy in your own fair house,
Remember all poor men that are abroad,
That Christ, who gave this roof, prepare for thee
Eternal dwelling in the house of God.

More than wages
John Gother

John Gother lived in the 17th century, dying in 1704. He was ordained in 1668 and acted as chaplain at Warkworth Castle, Northamptonshire, producing many volumes of down-to-earth instruction and commentaries on the Scripture readings for the year. He showed a sympathetic understanding for the realities of the working life that most of his readers led.

It is too much to expect that married persons should live exempt from dislike, contentions or jealousies; and many difficulties cannot fail of giving them disturbance either from difference of humours, from disagreeable passions, from indiscretions, or the following such ways, as are unwarrantable and destructive of the common interest. And what is there to be depended on but only that grace, which Jesus Christ gives to those who call him to the marriage? It is this alone can prevent these inconveniences from growing to an excess, or give them strength to go through them with the patience and courage of Christians.

And how can they hope for this, who binding themselves in an engagement of this concern without ever consulting him and marrying without his orders, do in effect declare that they believe themselves in no want of his assistance for satisfying the obligations and bearing the difficulties of their state? It must be nothing less than an extraordinary mercy, if he leaves them not to themselves and their passions, and to all those inconveniences which are so frequently in a married life, and permits not in his justice that what they, with so much earnestness, sought for their temporal advantage, may prove their punishment, and even hell in this world, and be the way to another that is eternal.

Though the profession of virginity and a religious life has many advantages in it such as prepare the undertakers for the more frequent presence, and stricter union with Christ; yet, there is no lawful state or business of life, even of persons engaged in the world, in which Christ will not be present, and give his benediction to it, if those concerned are but solicitous to invite him to it. We have an encouragement for this practical belief, from the many instances set down in holy writ, of persons who have found Christ, and had both the comfort and blessing of his sacred presence. Peter, with some other of the apostles, found him whilst engaged in their trade of fishing; Zaccheus found him on the road; the Samaritan woman at the well, when she was fetching water for her family; the blind man when he was begging; the sick man near the pond side taking care for his health; Magdalen at an entertainment; the lame man in the temple.

And what were all these occurrences? Not the effect of chance, but the appointments of providence, for the comfort of Christians in all conditions, that they might not disquiet themselves under any circumstances, as if they were not in any way of finding Christ or working out their salvation; but to be their assurance, that if the hurry of necessary business gives little opportunity for prayer or recollection, yet they may find Christ present with them, even in their business, as they will be but solicitous to invite him; the tradesman may find him in his shop, the labourer at his work, the plowman in the field, the porter in the streets, the traveller on the road, the servant in the kitchen, at the wash-bowl or spit, those that are sick by their bedside, and the afflicted in all their distress.

All this depends only on good management, and it being so much the Christian's interest to learn it, especially of those who are obliged to labour, I wish they would take St Francis Sales for their master, who in his Introduction to the Devout Life (Part III, chapter 35), teaches this lesson so well that the best advice I can give them, is to read it every week, that so they may become perfect in it, and make this advantage of all their labours, as not only to work for bread, but also for a better recompence, which is life everlasting.

The method of practising it must be in making an offering of every thing they do to God. He that has so expressly declared the acceptance of the widow's mite, and the value of a cup of cold water given in his name, has in this put it beyond all doubt, that there is nothing in itself so inconsiderable, but, if undertaken and performed in His name, will be accepted by him, in order to the obtaining from him an eternal recompence. And if every thing, even the ordinary actions of human life, as of eating and drinking according to St Paul's advice, may be thus consecrated to God, and have a part in the purchase; with much more reason, may the labours of those that work daily for bread be brought under this head. For however straitness of fortune may render them necessary; yet they may be undertaken – First, as a charity due to themselves or family; Secondly, as an act of justice, to satisfy the obligation they have of providing for those under their care. And these being duties enjoined them by God himself, they may the more easily be begun in his name, and be offered to him, as a sacrifice of obedience to his commands. And if they take all possible care to be faithful in them, this fidelity must have place among Christian virtues; and is one of those to which Christ has promised a reward; for he that shall be faithful in small matters, shall be set over greater.

And since all services, and laborious employments, have something difficult in them whether it be in the labour itself or in the circumstances of giving attendance to it – as in early rising, or sitting up late, or in tedious waiting; or in denying nature many satisfactions to which it is inclined and others take; or in serving nice and disagreeable humours; or in undeserved reproofs; or in being subject to impertinencies; or in cross accidents etc. – there is not one of these which may not be embraced, in compliance with the will of God, be made the exercise of daily patience and humility, and be accepted as a penance of their sins due from the justice of God.

Now if Christians would learn this lesson, is it not plain, that in doing only that to which they are otherwise obliged, they would make their lives the exercise of the greatest virtues, of charity, justice, patience, humility and penance. And who can doubt, but that Christ would be then with them, to give a blessing to their labours, and make them a sacrifice acceptable to God? Thus certainly it might be. And is it not a matter of pity, that this lesson is not more universally practised amongst servants, and labouring Christians; who live generally so little concerned for their greatest interest, that working hard all the year for poor wages, they offer nothing of what they do to him, who has promised to be more bountiful in his rewards; and that having received their wages, they have all they can expect? This is very ill husbandry, such as we have all too much reason to lament in ourselves; and we cannot do better this day than beg a remedy for it.

Help us therefore, O God, and teach us to be wise; that having so many opportunities every day, of making offerings to thee, both of what we do, and what we suffer, we may improve the occasions for our eternal advantage.

A cheerful task
Charles Wesley

Charles Wesley (1707–88) early joined with his brother John in the work that led to the emergence of Methodism. Many of his 6000 or so hymns are still sung. This one first appeared in Hymns and Sacred Poems *(1749).*

Forth in thy Name, O Lord, I go
My daily labour to pursue;
Thee, only thee, resolved to know,
In all I think, or speak, or do.

The task thy wisdom hath assigned,
O let me cheerfully fulfill;
In all my works thy presence find,
And prove thy good and perfect will.

Thee may I set at my right hand,
Whose eyes my inmost substance see:
And labour on at thy command,
And offer all my works to thee.

Give me to bear thy easy yoke,
And every moment watch and pray;
And still to things eternal look,
And hasten to thy glorious Day.

Fain would I still for thee employ
Whate'er thy bounteous grace hath given,
Would run my course with even joy
And closely walk with thee to heaven.

Another self
Aelred

Aelred of Rievaulx (1109–66) was born at Hexham, Northumberland, but lived as a Cistercian monk at the recently founded abbey at Rievaulx in York-shire, the ruins of which stand in the beautiful countryside as a poignant remin-der of a peaceful vocation spent praising God. Aelred's book Spiritual Friendship *incorporates much of Cicero's appreciation of non-sexual friend-ship, and then the Christian writer grafts the supernatural on to the natural gift.*

What happiness, what security, what joy to have someone to whom you dare to speak on terms of equality as to another self; one to whom you need have no fear to confess your failings; one to whom you can unblushingly make known what progress you have made in the spiritual life; one to whom you can entrust all the secrets of your heart and before whom you can place all your plans! What, therefore, is more pleasant than so to unite to oneself the spirit of another and of two to form one, that no boasting is thereafter to be feared, no suspicion to be dreaded, no correction of one by the other to cause pain, no praise on the part of one to bring a charge of adulation from the other.

'A friend,' says the Wise Man, 'is the medicine of life.' 'Excellent, indeed, is that saying. For medicine is not more powerful or more efficacious for our wounds in all our temporal needs than the possession of a friend who meets every misfortune joyfully, so that, as the Apostle says, shoulder to shoulder, they bear one another's burdens.' Even more – each one carries his own injuries even more lightly than that of his friend.

Friendship, therefore, heightens the joys of prosperity and mitigates the sorrows of adversity by dividing and sharing them. Hence, the best medicine in life is a friend. Even the philosophers took pleasure in the thought: not even water, nor the sun, nor fire do we use in more instances than a friend. In every action, in every pursuit, in certainty, in doubt, in every event and fortune of whatever sort, in private and in public, in every deliberation, at home and abroad, everywhere friendship is found to be appreciated, a friend a necessity, a friend's service a thing of utility. 'Wherefore, friends,' says Tullius, 'though absent are present, though poor are rich, though weak are strong, and what seems stranger still – though dead are alive.'

And so it is that the rich prize friendship as their glory, the exiles as their native land, the poor as their wealth, the sick as their medicine, the dead as their life, the healthy as their charm, the weak as their strength and the strong as their prize. So great are the distinction, memory, praise and affection that accompany friends that their lives are adjudged worthy of praise and their death rated as precious. And, a thing even more excellent than all these considerations, friendship is a stage bordering upon that perfection which consists in the love and knowledge of God, so that man from being a friend of his fellow man becomes the friend of God, according to the words of the Saviour in the Gospel: 'I will not now call you servants, but my friends.'

Like the useful bee
Jeremy Taylor

Jeremy Taylor (1613–67) had been chaplain to the supporter of Charles I, Archbishop Laud, who was executed in 1645. During the Commonwealth of Oliver Cromwell, Taylor lay low in Wales, building up a store of his remarkable sermons. When the king came back in, in 1660, Taylor was made a bishop. The extract below comes from his celebrated sermon 'The Marriage Ring'.

Here is the proper scene of piety and patience, of the duty of parents and the charity of relatives; here kindness is spread abroad, and love is united and made firm as a centre: marriage is the nursery of heaven; the virgin sends prayers to God, but she carries but one soul to Him; but the state of marriage fills up the numbers of the elect, and hath in it the labour of love, and the delicacies of friendship, the blessing of society, and the union of hands and hearts; it hath in it less of beauty, but more of safety, than the single life; it hath more care, but less danger; it is more merry, and more sad; is fuller of sorrows, and fuller of joys; it lies under more burdens, but it is supported by all the strengths of love and charity, and those burdens are delightful. Marriage is the mother of the world, and preserves kingdoms, and fills cities, and churches, and heaven itself.

Celibate, like the fly in the heart of an apple, dwells in a perpetual sweetness, but sits alone, and is confined and dies in singularity; but marriage, like the useful bee, builds a house and gathers sweetness from every flower, and labours and unites into societies and republics, and sends out colonies, and feeds the world with delicacies, and obeys their king, and keeps order, and exercises many virtues, and promotes the interest of mankind, and is that state of good things to which God hath designed the present constitution of the world.

Pregnancy as work of art
Francis de Sales

Francis de Sales (1567–1622) had the difficult task of ministering as a Catholic in the diocese of Geneva, the headquarters of Calvinism. He taught that a life of friendship with God belonged to lay men and women as much as to the clergy and religious orders. The letter here is one of many to married women who sought his advice.

September 29 1620 My dearest daughter, I am not at all surprised that your heart seems a little heavy and sluggish. A delicate body weighed down by the burden of pregnancy, weakened by the labour of carrying a child, troubled with many pains, cannot allow the heart to be so lively, so active, so ready in its operations, but all this in no way injures the acts of that higher part of the soul, which are as agreeable to God as they could be in the midst of all the gladnesses in the world – yes, more agreeable in all truth, as being done with more labour and effort. But these acts of the soul are not so agreeable to the person who makes them, because they do not come from the sensible part and are not so much felt, or so pleasant to us.

My dearest daughter, we must not be unjust and require from ourselves what is not in ourselves. When troubled in body and health, we must not exact from our souls more than acts of submission and acceptance of labour, and holy unions of our will to the good pleasure of God, which are formed in the highest region of the spirit. As for exterior actions we must manage and do them the best we can. Have patience then with yourself. Let your superior part bear the disorder of the inferior; and often offer to the eternal glory of our Creator the little creature in whose formation he has willed to make you his fellow-worker.

My dearest daughter, we have at Annecy a Capuchin painter who, as you may think, only paints for God and his holy building: and though while working he has to pay such close attention that he cannot pray at the same time, and though this occupies and even tires his spirit, still he works with good heart for the glory of the Lord, and the hope that these pictures will excite many of the faithful to praise God and to bless his goodness.

Well, my dear daughter, your child will be a living image of the Divine majesty; but while your soul, your strength, your natural vigour is occupied with this work, it must grow weary, and tired, and you cannot at the same time perform your ordinary exercises so actively and so gaily. You rather suffer lovingly this tiredness and heaviness, in consideration of the honour which God will receive from your work. It is your image which will be placed in the eternal temple of the heavenly Jerusalem, and will be eternally regarded with pleasure by God, by angels and by men. And the saints will praise God for it, and you also will praise him when you see it there.

When loved and happy meet
John Clare

John Clare (1793–1864) was poor and went mad, but neither prevented him from sharply observing the beauties of his Northamptonshire countryside and putting them into poetry. He had a great fondness for children, and though he knew that labour was hard, he relished the homeliness of rural life. He wrote the poem below in 1844 in Northampton County Asylum.

Evening Hours

> The cool of the evening is the hour of Heaven:
> The time Earth holds communion with the sky,
> When angels' thoughts to evening walks are given,
> And whispering in the hedges round us lie,
> Like Heaven talking in our infancy,

One sweet soft cupola appears, the clouds,
Purple, and rose, and gold, far west do lie;
May blossoms on the hedges sleep in crowds
And evening rests in day's retiring shrouds.
Day's reiterative toils repose, the hour
When infants cradle on the mother's breast,
Likes roses in the dews, yet half in flower;
While day yet lingers in the golden west
Beasts to their sheds, the small birds to their nest,
Clouds to the trees, dews to the flowers are given;
The dews like cordials fall on toil, and rest.
The dog-rose glistens with the dews of even
And peace reposes in the midst of Heaven.
It is the hour the lover meets his heart,
At least the maid who keeps it in her breast:
It is the hour that lovers will impart
Their heart's own secret, ere the hour of rest:
It is the hour the social life likes best,
When neighbours, children, wife and husband meet,
The hour when blessings they are doubly bless'd,
The hour when dews are brush'd by lovers' feet,
The soft sweet hour when lov'd and happy meet.

A husband restored
Anne Bradstreet

*Anne Bradstreet (1612–72) was born in Northampton but in 1630 went with
her husband to America, settling in Massachusetts, of which he was to become
the governor. They were strong Puritans. In 1650 a volume of her poetry was
published in England by the initiative of her brother-in-law. But most of her
poetry was written as a means of meditative prayer.*

For the restoration of my dear husband from a burning ague, June 1 1661

Whence fears and sorrows me beset
Then didst Thou rid me out;
When heart did faint and spirits quail,
Thou comfortst me about.

Thou rais'st him up I feared to lose,
Regav'st me him again,
Distempers Thou didst chase away,
With strength didst him sustain.

My thankful heart with pen record
The goodness of thy God,
Let thy obedience testify
He taught thee by His rod.

And with His staff did thee support
That thou by both may'st learn,
And 'twixt the good and evil way
At last, thou might'st discern.

Praises to Him who hath not left
My soul as destitute,
Nor turned His ear away from me,
But granted hath my suit.

To be is good

Astonishment at existence
G.K. Chesterton

G.K. Chesterton (1874–1936) reacted against the pessimism and scepticism of the late Victorians among whom he grew up. Although he earned his living as a journalist he was more interested in the reality underneath facts, always having the ability to tear the heart out of any book he read. A liberal in politics he had a visceral attraction to orthodoxy in philosophy. Something of his attitude is shown in Orthodoxy *(1909) and in the novel* The Man Who Was Thursday *(1907). He became a Catholic only in 1922. The passage here comes from his* Autobiography *(1936).*

What surprises me in looking back on youth, and even on boyhood, is the extreme rapidity with which it can think its way back to fundamental things; and even to the denial of fundamental things. At a very early age I had thought my way back to thought itself. It is a very dreadful thing to do; for it may lead to thinking that there is nothing but thought. At this time I did not very clearly distinguish between dreaming and waking; not only as a mood, but as a metaphysical doubt, I felt as if everything might be a dream. It was as if I had myself projected the universe from within, with all its trees and stars; and that is so near to the notion of being God that it is manifestly even nearer to going mad.

Yet I was not mad, in any medical or physical sense; I was simply carrying the scepticism of my time as far as it would go. And I soon found it would go a great deal further than most of the sceptics went. While dull atheists came and explained to me that there was nothing but matter, I listened with a sort of calm horror of detachment, suspecting that there was nothing but mind. I have always felt that there was something thin and third-rate about materialists and materialism ever since. The atheist told me so pompously that he did not believe there was any God; and there were moments when I did not even believe there was any atheist.

And as with mental, so with moral extremes. There is something truly menacing in the thought of how quickly I could imagine the maddest, when I had never committed the mildest crime. Something may have been due to the atmosphere of the Decadents, and their perpetual hints of the luxurious horrors of paganism; but I am not disposed to dwell much on that defence; I suspect I manufactured most of my morbidities for myself. But anyhow, it is true that there was a time when I had reached that condition of moral anarchy within, in which a man says, in the words of Wilde, that 'Atys with the blood-stained knife were better than the thing I am.' I have never indeed felt the faintest temptation to the particular madness of Wilde; but I could at this time imagine the worst and wildest disproportions and distortions of more normal passion; the point is that the whole mood was overpowered and oppressed with a sort of congestion of imagination. As Bunyan, in his morbid period, described himself as prompted to utter blasphemies, I had an overpowering impulse to record or draw horrible ideas and images; plunging deeper and deeper as in a blind spiritual suicide. I had never heard of Confession, in any serious sense, in those days; but that is what is really needed in such cases. I fancy they are not uncommon cases.

Anyhow, the point is here that I dug quite low enough to discover the devil; and even in some dim way to recognize the devil. At least I never, even in this first vague and sceptical stage, indulged very much in the current arguments about the relativity of evil or the unreality of sin. Perhaps, when I eventually emerged as a sort of a theorist, and was described as an Optimist, it was because I was one of the few people in that world of diabolism who really believed in devils.

In truth, the story of what was called my Optimism was rather odd. When I had been for some time in these, the darkest depths of the contemporary pessimism, I had a strong inward impulse to revolt; to dislodge this incubus or throw off this nightmare. But as I was still thinking the thing out by myself, with little help from philosophy and no real help from religion, I invented a rudimentary and makeshift mystical theory of my own. It was substantially this: that even mere existence, reduced to its most primary limits, was extraordinary enough to be exciting. Anything was magnificent as compared with nothing. Even if the very daylight were a dream, it was a day-dream; it was not a nightmare. The mere fact that one could wave one's arms and legs about (or those dubious external objects in the landscape which were called one's arms and legs) showed that it had not the mere paralysis of a nightmare. Or if it was a nightmare, it was an enjoyable nightmare. In fact, I had wandered to a position not very far from the phrase of my Puritan grandfather, when he said that he would thank God for his creation if he were a lost soul.

I hung on to the remains of religion by one thin thread of thanks. I thanked whatever gods might be, not like Swinburne, because no life lived for ever, but because any life lived at all; not, like Henley, for my unconquerable soul (for I have never been so optimistic about my own soul as all that), but for my own soul and my own body, even if they could be conquered.

This way of looking at things, with a sort of mystical minimum of gratitude, was of course, to some extent assisted by those few of the fashionable writers who were not pessimists; especially by Walt Whitman, by Browning and by Stevenson; Browning's 'God must be glad one loves his world so much,' or Stevenson's 'belief in the ultimate decency of things'. But I do not think it is too much to say that I took it in a way of my own; even if it was a way I could not see clearly or make very clear. What I meant, whether or no I managed to say it, was this: that no man knows how much he is an optimist, even when he calls himself a pessimist, because he has not really measured the depths of his debt to whatever created him and enabled him to call himself anything. At the back of our brains, so to speak, there was a forgotten blaze or burst of astonishment at our own existence.

39

The object of the artistic and spiritual life was to dig for this sub-merged sunrise of wonder; so that a man sitting in a chair might suddenly understand that he was actually alive, and be happy.

I only know I am
John Clare

John Clare (1793–1864) went through hard experiences during his years of madness. All the time, though, he crafted careful poetry, as with the sonnet below. He managed to express the determination with which he clung on to reality. This poem may be read as a complementary piece to his more famous 'I am'.

I feel I am, I only know I am,
And plod upon the earth and dull and void:
Earth's prison chilled my body with its dram
Of dullness, and my soaring thoughts destroyed.
I fled to solitude from passion's dream,
But strife pursued – I only know I am.
I was a being created in the race
Of men, disdaining bounds of place and time,
A spirit that could travel o'er the space
Of earth and heaven, like a thought sublime –
Tracing creation, like my Maker free, –
A soul unshackled – like eternity:
Spurning earth's vain and soul debasing thrall –
But now I only know I am, – that's all.

All shall be well
Julian of Norwich

Julian (born 1342) was a woman who made her home as an anchoress or hermit in a cell next to the church of St Julian in Norwich. She was plainly level-headed, giving sensible advice to her more neurotic contemporary Margery

Kemp. In her life of prayer she discerned sixteen special personal revelations or 'showings' from Jesus, of which those below form the twelfth and thirteenth in her book Revelations of Divine Love. *It is worth remarking that the word 'shall' in the phrase 'all shall be well' indicates grammatically determination or emphasis on the part of the speaker.*

After this our Lord showed himself more glorious in my sight than I had seen him before and I was taught that our soul shall never have rest till it comes to him, with the knowledge that he is fulness of joy and courtesy, our home and utter happiness and life itself.

Our Lord Jesus said to me repeatedly: 'It is I, it is I; it is I that am highest; I that you love, I that you enjoy, I that you servest; I that you long for, I that you desire, I that you mean, I that am all. I of whom Holy Church preaches and teaches you, I that show myself here to you.' His many words passed my understanding and comprehension and all my powers. They seem to me so high, for in them is comprehended – I cannot tell how much – but the joy that I saw in the showing of them goes beyond all that heart may wish for and soul may desire. The words are not all declared here, but everyone, according to the grace that God gives him to understand and love, receives them according to our Lord's meaning.

After this, our Lord brought to my mind the longing for him that I had before. And I saw that nothing hindered me but sin. And this, I saw, applied generally to us all. I thought, 'If there had been no sin, we should all have been clean and like our Lord, as he made us.'

In my folly, before this time, I often wondered why, with the great foreseeing wisdom of God, the beginnings of sin had not been prevented; for then, I thought, all should have been well. This stirring of mind should have been abandoned, but nevertheless I underwent much mourning and sorrow because of it, beyond all reason and discretion.

But Jesus, who in this vision told me all that I needed to know, answered in these terms, saying: 'It was necessary that there should have been sin; but all shall be well, and all shall be well, and all manner of thing shall be well.'

41

In this naked word 'sin', our Lord brought to my mind generally – all that is not good, and the shameful treatment and humiliation that he bore for us in this life, and his dying; and all the pains and sufferings of all his creatures, spiritual and bodily (for we are all humiliated in part, and we shall be rid of all things in following our Master, Jesus, till we are fully purged, that is to say, till we are rid of body of death and of all our inward affections that are not good). Seeing this, all pains that ever were or ever shall be, I realize that the Passion of Christ was the most painful, more painful than any other. All this was revealed in a moment, and it quickly turned into comfort: for our good Lord did not want my soul to be frightened by this terrible sight.

But I did not see sin: for I believe it has no kind of substance or element of being, and that it can be known only by the pain it causes. And so pain is something, it seems to me, that is temporary; for it purges us and makes us know ourselves and to ask for mercy. For the Passion of our Lord is comfort to us against all this, and so is his blessed will.

And because of the tender love that our good Lord has for all that shall be saved, he brings comfort readily and sweetly, saying: 'It is true that sin is the cause of all this pain; but all shall be well, and all shall be well, and all manner of thing shall be well.'

These words were said most tenderly, not in any way blaming me, or any that shall be saved. So it would be most ungrateful to blame God or exclaim to him because of my sin, since he does not blame me for sin.

In these words that were spoken I saw a marvellous and high mystery hidden in God, and this mystery he will make known to us openly in heaven. In the understanding of it we shall truly see why he allowed sin to happen. And in the seeing of this mystery we shall have endless joy in our Lord God.

Attitude

Living in the sun
John Henry Newman

John Henry Newman (1801–90) sought the truths of Christianity among the ancient Fathers of the Church. His spiritual journey from the Church of England to the Catholic Church is well known, but one of his dicta was 'to live is to change', by which he meant continuing development and growth towards God. He has been represented as being somehow weedy, so it is pleasant to find a sermon, preached for Septuagesima (the third Sunday before Lent) in his Anglican days, that urges the people to eat, drink and be merry .

Gloom is no Christian temper; that repentance is not real which has not love in it; that self-chastisement is not acceptable, which is not sweetened by faith and cheerfulness. We must live in sunshine, even when we sorrow; we must live in God's presence, we must not shut ourselves up in our own hearts, even when we are reckoning up our past sins.

These thoughts are suitable on this day, when we first catch a sight, as it were, of the Forty Days of Lent. If God then gives us grace to repent, it is well; if He enables us to chasten heart and body, to Him be praise; and for that very reason, while we do so, we must not cease rejoicing in Him. All through Lent we must rejoice, while we afflict ourselves. Though 'many be called; but few chosen'; though all run in the race, but 'one receiveth the prize'; though we must 'so run that we may obtain'; though we must be 'temperate in all things', and 'keep under our body and bring it into subjection, lest we be castaways'; yet through God alone we can do this; and while He is with us, we cannot but be joyful; for His absence only is a cause for sorrow.

The Three Holy Children are said to have stood up in the midst of the fire, and to have called on all the works of God to rejoice with

43

them; on sun and moon, stars of heaven, nights and days, showers and dew, frost and cold, lightnings and clouds, mountains and hills, green things upon the earth, seas and floods, fowls of the air, beasts and cattle, and children of men, to praise and bless the Lord, and magnify Him for ever. We have no such trial as theirs; we have no such awful suspense as theirs, when they entered the burning fiery furnace; we attempt for the most part what we know we begin, what we think we can go through.

We can neither instance their faith nor equal their rejoicing; yet we can imitate them so far as to look abroad into this fair world, which God made 'very good', while we mourn over the evil which Adam brought into it; to hold communion with what we see there, while we seek Him who is invisible; to admire it, while we abstain from it; to acknowledge God's love, while we deprecate His wrath; to confess that, many as are our sins, His grace is greater. Our sins are more in number than the hairs of our head; yet even the hairs of our head are all numbered by Him. He counts our sins, and, as He counts, so can He forgive; for that reckoning, great though it be, comes to an end; but His mercies fail not and His Son's merits are infinite.

Let us, then, on this day, dwell upon a thought which it will be a duty to carry with us through Lent, the thought of the blessings and mercies of which our present life is made up. St Paul said that he had all; and abounded, and was full; and this, in a day of persecution. Surely, if we have but religious hearts and eyes, we too must confess that our daily and hourly blessing in this life are not less than his. Let us recount some of them.

1. First, then, we ought to bless and praise God that we have the gift of life. By this I mean, not merely that we live, but for those blessings which are included in the notion of our living. He has made life in its very nature to imply the existence of certain blessings which are themselves a happiness, and which bring it to pass that, in spite of all evils, life in itself, except in rare cases, cannot be otherwise than desirable. We cannot live without the means of life; without the means of life we should die; and the means of life are means of pleasure. It might have so been ordered that life could not have been

sustained without the use of such means as were indifferent, neither pleasurable nor painful, – or of means which were even painful; as in the case of illness or disease, when we actually find that we cannot preserve it without painful remedies.

Now, supposing the ordinary ways of preserving it had been what are now but extraordinary: supposing food were medicine; supposing wounds or blows imparted health and strength. But it is not so. On the contrary, life consists in things pleasant; it is sustained by blessings. And, moreover, the Gospel, by a solemn grant, guarantees these things to us.

After the Flood, God Almighty condescended to promise that there never should be such a flood again; that seed-time and harvest should not fail. He ratified the stability of nature by His own Word, and by that Word it is upheld. And in like manner He has, in a special way, guaranteed to us in the Gospel that law of nature whereby good and pleasant gifts are included in our idea of life, and life becomes a blessing. Did He so will, He might sustain us Christians, not by bread only, but by every word that proceedeth out of His mouth. But He has not done so. He has pledged to us those ordinary means of sustenance which we naturally like: 'bread shall be given us; our water shall be sure'; 'all these things shall be added unto us'.

He has not indeed promised us what the world calls its great prizes; He has not promised us those goods, so called, of which the goodness depends on the imagination; He has not promised us large estates, magnificent domains, houses like palaces, sumptuous furniture, retainers and servants, chariots and horses, rank, name, credit, popularity, power, the deference of others, the indulgence of our wills, luxuries, sensual enjoyments. These, on the contrary, He denies us and, withal, He declares, that, specious and inviting as they are, really they are evil. But still He has promised that this shall be His rule; – that thus shall it be fulfilled to us as His ordinary providence, viz. – that life shall not be a burden to us, but a blessing, and shall contain more to comfort than to afflict.

And giving us as much as this, He bids us be satisfied with it; He bids us confess that we 'have all' when we have so much: that we 'abound' when we have enough; He promises us food, raiment, and lodging; and He bids us, 'having food and raiment, therewith to be content'. He bids us be content with those gifts, and withal unsolicitous about them; tranquil, secure, and confident, because He has promised them; He bids us be sure that we shall have so much, and not be disappointed that it is no more. Such is His merciful consideration of us; He does not separate us from this world, though He calls us out of it; He does not reject our old nature when He gives us a new one, He does but redeem it from the curse, and purify it from the infection which came through Adam, and is none of His.

He especially blesses the creation to our use, though we be regenerate. 'Every creature of God,' says the Apostle, 'is good, and nothing to be refused, if it be received with thanksgiving, for it is sanctified by the word of God and prayer.' He does not bid us renounce the creation, but associates us with the most beautiful portions of it. He likens us to the flowers with which He has ornamented the earth, and to the birds that live solitary under heaven, and makes them the type of a Christian. He denies us Solomon's regal magnificence, to unite us to the lilies of the field and the fowls of the air. 'Take no thought for your life, what ye shall eat or what ye shall drink, nor yet for your body, what ye shall put on. Is not the life more than meat, and the body than raiment? Behold the fowls of the air, for they sow not, neither do they reap, nor gather into barns; yet your heavenly Father feedeth them. Are ye not much better than they? . . . And why take ye thought for raiment? Consider the lilies of the field, how they grow; they toil not, neither do they spin; and yet I say unto you, that even Solomon in all his glory was not arrayed like one of these.'

Here then, surely, is a matter for joy and thankfulness at all seasons, and not the least at times when, with a religious forbearance, and according to the will of the Giver, not from thanklessness but from prudence, we, for a while, more or less withhold from ourselves His good gifts. Then, of all times, when we think it right to suspend our use of the means of life, so far as may not hurt that life, His gift, and to prove how pleasant is the using them by the pain of abstaining from them, – now especially, my brethren, in the weeks in prospect, when we shall be called on to try ourselves, as far as may be, by hunger, or cold, or watching, or seclusion, that we may be brought nearer to God, – let us now thank God that He has not put us into an evil world, or subjected us to a cruel master, but has given us a continual record of His own perfections in all that lies around us.

Alas! It will be otherwise hereafter with those whom God puts out of His sight for ever. Their world will be evil; their life will be death; their rulers will be the devil and his angels; flames of fire and the lake of brimstone will be their meat and drink; the heaven above them will be brass; their earth will be dust and ashes; the blood in their veins will be as molten lead. Fearful thought! which it is not right to do more than glance at. Let us utter it, and pass by.

Rather it is for us to rejoice that we are still in the light of His countenance, on His good earth, and under His warm sun. Let us thank Him that He gives us the fruits of the earth in their season; that He gives us 'food out of the earth, and wine that maketh glad the heart of man, and oil to make him a cheerful countenance, and bread to strengthen man's heart'. Thus was it with our fathers of old time; thus is it with us now. After Abraham had fought with the kings, Melchizedek brought forth bread and wine to refresh him. The Angels who visited him made themselves men, and ate of the calf which he dressed for them. Isaac blessed Jacob after the savoury meat. Joseph's brethren ate and drank, and were merry with him. The seventy elders went up Mount Sinai with Moses, Aaron, Nadab, and Abihu, and they saw God, and moreover 'did eat and drink'. David, after his repentance, had 'bread set before him, and he did eat'. When Elijah went for his life, and requested that he might die, 'an Angel touched him, and said unto him, Arise and eat'; and he did eat and drink, once and twice, and lay down to sleep between his meals; and when he arose, he 'went in the strength of that meat forty days and forty nights unto Horeb the mount of God'. St Paul also, after his conversion and baptism, 'received meat and was strengthened'.

2. Again, what a great blessing is that gift, of which I have just spoken in Elijah's case, the gift of sleep. Almighty God does not

suffer us to be miserable for a long while together, even when He afflicts us; but He breaks our trial into portions; takes us out of this world ever and anon, and gives us a holy-day time, like children at school, in an unknown and mysterious country.

All this then must be borne in mind, in reflecting on these solemn and sobering truths concerning the Christian's calling, which it is necessary often to insist upon. It is often said, and truly, that the Christian is born to trouble, – that sorrow is the rule with him, and pleasure the exception. But when this is said, it is with reference to seasons, circumstances, events, such things as are adventitious and additional to the gift of life itself. The Christian's lot is one of sorrow, but, as the regenerate life with him is happiness, so is the gift of natural life also. We live, therefore we are happy; upon this life of ours come joys and sorrows; and in proportion as we are favourites of God, it is sorrow that comes, not joy.

Still after all considered in ourselves, that we live; that God breathes in us; that we exist in Him; that we think and act; that we have the means of life; that we have food, and sleep, and raiment, and lodging; and that we are not lonely, but in God's Church, and are sure of brethren by the very token of our having a Father which is in heaven; so far, rejoicing is the very condition of our being, and all pain is little more than external, not reaching to our inmost heart. So far all men almost are on a level; seasons of sickness excepted. Even delicate health and feebleness of life does not preclude these pleasures. And as to seasons of sickness, or even long and habitual pain or disease, the good Lord can compensate for them in His own way by extraordinary supplies of grace, as in early times He made even the torments of Christians in persecution literally pleasant to them. He who so ordered it, that even the red-hot iron did feel pleasant to the Martyrs after a while, cannot fail of means to support His servants when life becomes a burden.

But, generally speaking, it is a happiness, and that to all ranks. High and low, rich and poor, have the same refreshment in their pilgrimage. Hunger is as pleasantly appeased by the low as by the high, on coarse fare as on delicate. Sleep is equally the comfort and recruiting of rich and poor. We eat, drink, and sleep, whether we are in sorrow or in joy, in anxiety or in hope. Our natural life is the type of our spiritual life, and thus, in a literal as well as higher sense, we may bless Him 'who saveth our life from destruction, and crowneth us with mercy and loving-kindness; who satisfieth our mouth with good things making us young and lusty as an eagle.'

Cheerfulness
Mother Teresa

Mother Teresa of Calcutta (1910–97) taught her followers to love the poor-est of the poor, 'the unwanted, the unloved, the uncared for', of any religion, because that is to love Jesus.

God loves a cheerful giver;
he gives most who gives with joy.

The best way to show your gratitude
to God and people is to
accept everything with joy.

A sister filled with joy is like
the sunshine of God's love,
the hope of eternal happiness,
the flame of burning love.

Never let anything so fill you with
sorrow as to make you forget
the joy of the risen Christ.

Not as the hedgehog
John Tillotson

John Tillotson (1630–94) became Archbishop of Canterbury in 1691 after William Sancroft was deposed for refusing to take the oath to William III when he took the throne. Tillotson used a plain style for his sermons which won them hearers and a good sale in printed collections. This extract from a sermon on 'The example of Jesus in doing good' makes the point that doing good brings lasting pleasure.

Those who are of a narrow and envious spirit, of a mean and sordid disposition, love to contract themselves within themselves, and like the hedgehog to shoot out their quills at everyone that comes near them. They take care of nobody but themselves, and foolishly think their own happiness the greater because they have it alone and to themselves.

But the noblest and most heavenly dispositions think themselves happiest when others share with them in their happiness. Of all beings GOD is the farthest removed from envy, and the nearer any creature approacheth to him in blessedness the farther is it off from this hellish quality and disposition. It is the temper of the devil to grudge happiness to others; he envied that man should be in paradise when he was cast out of heaven.

Other perfections are (as one says) of a more melancholic and solitary disposition, and shine brightest when they are alone, or attained to but by a few. Once make them common and they lose their lustre. But it is the nature of goodness to communicate itself, and the farther it spreads the more glorious it is. GOD reckons it as one of his most glorious titles, the brightest gem in his diadem, 'the LORD mighty to save'. He delights not to shew his sovereignty in ruining the innocent and destroying helpless creatures; but in rescuing them out of the jaws of hell and destruction. To the devil belongs the title of the destroyer.

Without this quality of goodness all other perfections would change their nature, and lose their excellency. Great power and wisdom would be terrible, and raise nothing but dread and suspicion in us; for power without goodness would be tyranny and oppression, and wisdom would become craft and treachery. A being endued with knowledge and power, and yet wanting goodness, would be nothing else but an irresistible evil, and an omnipotent mischief. We admire knowledge, and are afraid of power, and suspect wisdom but we can heartily love nothing but goodness, or such perfections as are in conjunction with it. For knowledge and power may be in a nature most contrary to GOD's; the devil hath these perfections in an excelling degree. When all is done, nothing argues a great and generous mind but only goodness; which is a propension and disposition to make others happy, and a readiness to do them all the good offices we can.

Secondly, to do good is the most pleasant employment in the world. It is natural; and whatever is so is delightful. We do like our selves whenever we relieve the wants and distresses of others. And therefore this virtue among all other hath peculiarly entitled itself to the name of humanity. We answer our own nature, and obey our reason, and shew ourselves men, in shewing mercy to the miserable. Whenever we consider the evils and afflictions of others, we do with the greatest reason collect our duty from our nature and inclination, and make our own wishes and desires and expectations from others a law and rule to our selves. And this is pleasant, to follow our nature, and to gratify the importunate dictates of our own reason. So that the benefits we do to others are not more welcome to them that receive them, than they are delightful to us that do them.

We ease our own nature and bowels whenever we help and relieve those who are in want and necessity. As on the contrary, no man that hath not divested himself of humanity can be cruel and hard-hearted to others without feeling some pain to himself. There is no sensual pleasure in the world comparable to the delight and satisfaction that a good man takes in doing good. This Cato in Tully boasts of as the great comfort and joy of his old age, 'that nothing was more pleasant to him than the conscience of a well-spent life, and the remembrance of many benefits and kindnesses done to others'. Sensual pleasures are not lasting, but presently vanish and expire: but that is not the worst of them, they leave a sting behind them, as the pleasure goes off – *succedit frigida cura*.

Sadness and melancholy come in the place of it, guilt and trouble and repentance follow it. But the pleasure of doing good remains after a thing is done, the thoughts of it lie easy in our minds, and the reflection upon it afterwards does for ever minister joy and delight to us. In a word, that frame of mind which inclines us to do good is the very temper and disposition of happiness.

Solomon, after all his experience of worldly pleasures, pitches at last upon this as the greatest felicity of human life, and the only good use that is to be made of a prosperous and plentiful fortune: 'I know that there is no good in them, but for a man to rejoice and do good in his life' (Ecclesiastes, 3:12). And one greater than Solomon hath said, that 'it is more blessed to give than to receive'.

Twenty tips
Sydney Smith

Sydney Smith (1771–1845) was noted for his wit. Though a clergyman of the Church of England he was a Whig who favoured toleration.

To Lady Georgiana Morpeth
Foston, Feb 16th, 1820

Dear Lady Georgiana, . . . Nobody has suffered more from low spirits than I have done – so I feel for you.
- 1st. Live as well as you dare.
- 2nd. Go into the shower-bath with a small quantity of water at a temperature low enough to give you a slight sensation of cold, 75 degrees or 80 degrees.
- 3rd. Amusing books.
- 4th. Short views of human life – not further than dinner or tea.
- 5th. Be as busy as you can.

6th. See as much as you can of those friends who respect and like you.

7th. And of those acquaintances who amuse you.

8th. Make no secret of low spirits to your friends, but talk of them freely – they are always worse for dignified concealment.

9th. Attend to the effects tea and coffee produce upon you.

10th. Compare your lot with that of other people.

11th. Don't expect too much from human life – a sorry business at the best.

12th. Avoid poetry, dramatic representations (except comedy), music, serious novels, melancholy sentimental people and everything likely to excite feeling or emotion not ending in active benevolence.

13th. Do good, and endeavour to please everybody of every degree.

14th. Be as much as you can in the open air without fatigue.

15th. Make the room where you commonly sit gay and pleasant.

16th. Struggle by little and little against idleness.

17th. Don't be too severe upon yourself, or underrate yourself, but do yourself justice.

18th. Keep good blazing fires.

19th. Be firm and constant in the exercise of rational religion.

20th. Believe me, dear Lady Georgiana,

Very truly yours,
Sydney Smith

Twenty-one hints
Frederick Faber

Frederick Faber (1814–63) possessed remarkable energy and good will. Plunging into the Tractarian movement of the Church of England he soon found himself a Catholic and surrounded himself with followers in a religious order of his own devising. But he immediately threw himself into the Oratorian congregation that John Henry Newman introduced into England, with provoking consequences for poor Newman who never could tell what Faber meant to do next. Faber set up at the Brompton Oratory, prayed and wrote books and hymns and died exhausted.

Hints for valetudinarians

1. Not to aim at making long meditations.
2. Not to kneel for long together, but to pray in postures which do not incommode the body.
3. To avoid burdening yourself with many vocal prayers.
4. Not to perform spiritual exercises shortly after meals.
5. To avoid long church functions, as lassitude brings on indevotion.
6. To be much given to spiritual reading, and that pausingly, as a compensation for long mental prayer.
7. To go very frequently to Confession, and so make examen of conscience less onerous.
8. Not to have set times for more things than experience shows to be necessary.
9. To meditate chiefly on the Incarnation, not on the four last things and the like.
10. Never to attempt mortifications connected with eating or sleeping.
11. To devote yourself to ejaculatory prayer.
12. Never to keep a journal, or note down spiritual sentiments on paper.
13. To surround yourself with holy pictures and images.
14. To ask at all Communions for a childlike humility, and for the gift of the sensible Presence of God.
15. To think as seldom as possible of past sins.
16. To avoid solemnity of manner.
17. The government of the tongue is the great field of valetudinarian mortification.
18. Considerate gentleness to servants should be an especial virtue of valetudinarians.

19. Thanksgivings after, or preparations for Holy Communion, should not be prolonged when they require much effort.
20. Touchiness of temper and inordinate desire for sympathy must be guarded against.
21. If you have fixed mornings for Communion, do not scruple to change the morning if you feel unwell, or have a presentiment of unwellness.

Relearning happiness
Oscar Wilde

Oscar Wilde (1854–1900) with brilliancy and some absurdity furthered the claims of the aesthetic movement. In The Importance of Being Earnest *(1895) he constructed an eminently successful drama from a string of wittily conceived aperçus. By contrast* De Profundis, *published posthumously, from which the extract below is taken, examines the effect on his spirit of two years' imprisonment for gross indecency.*

I HAVE lain in prison for nearly two years. Out of my nature has come wild despair; an abandonment to grief that was piteous even to look at; terrible and impotent rage; bitterness and scorn; anguish that wept aloud; misery that could find no voice; sorrow that was dumb. I have passed through every possible mood of suffering. Better than Wordsworth himself I know what Wordsworth meant when he said:

> Suffering is permanent obscure and dark
> And has the nature of infinity.

But while there were times when I rejoiced in the idea that my sufferings were to be endless, I could not bear them to be without meaning. Now I find hidden somewhere away in my nature something that tells me that nothing in the whole world is meaningless, and suffering least of all. That something hidden away in my nature, like a treasure in a field, is Humility.

It is the last thing left in me, and the best: the ultimate discovery at which I have arrived, the starting point for a fresh development. It has come to me right out of myself, so I know that it has come at the proper time. It could not have come before, nor later. Had anyone told me of it, I would have rejected it. Had it been brought to me, I would have refused it. As I found it, I want to keep it. I must do so. It is the one thing that has in it the elements of life, of a new life; a *Vita Nuova* for me. Of all things it is the strangest; one cannot give it away and another may not give it to one. One cannot acquire it except by surrendering everything that one has. It is only when one has lost all things, that one knows that one possesses it.

Now I have realized that it is in me, I see quite clearly what I ought to do; in fact, must do. And when I use such a phrase as that, I need not say that I am not alluding to any external sanction or command. I admit none. I am far more of an individualist than I ever was. Nothing seems to me of the smallest value except what one gets out of oneself. My nature is seeking a fresh mode of self-realization. That is all I am concerned with. And the first thing that I have got to do is to free myself from any possible bitterness of feeling against the world. . . .

When first I was put into prison some people advised me to try and forget who I was. It was ruinous advice. It is only by realizing what I am that I have found comfort of any kind. Now I am advised by others to try on my release to forget that I have ever been in a prison at all. I know that would be equally fatal. It would mean that I would always be haunted by an intolerable sense of disgrace, and that those things that are meant for me as much as for anybody else – the beauty of the sun and moon, the pageant of the seasons, the music of daybreak and the silence of great nights, the rain falling through the leaves, or the dew creeping over the grass and making it silver – would all be tainted for me, and lose their healing power and their power of communicating joy. To regret one's own experiences is to arrest one's own development. To deny one's own experiences is to put a lie into the lips of one's own life. It is no less than a denial of the soul. . . .

Then I must learn how to be happy. Once I knew it, or thought I knew it, by instinct. It was always springtime once in my heart. My temperament was akin to joy. I filled my life to the very brim with pleasure, as one might fill a cup to the very brim with wine. Now I am approaching life from a completely new standpoint, and even to conceive happiness is often extremely difficult for me. I remember during my first term at Oxford reading in Pater's *Renaissance* – that book which has had such strange influence over my life – how Dante places low in the *Inferno* those who wilfully live in sadness; and going to the college library and turning to the passage in the *Divine Comedy* where beneath the dreary marsh lie those who were 'sullen in the sweet air', saying for ever and ever through their sighs –

> Tristi fummo
> Nell'aere dolce che dal sol s'allegra.

I knew the Church condemned *accidia*, but the whole idea seemed to me quite fantastic, just the sort of sin, I fancied, a priest who knew nothing about real life would invent. Nor could I understand how Dante, who says that 'sorrow remarries us to God', could have been so harsh to those who were enamoured of melancholy, if any such there really were. I had no idea that some day this would become to me one of the greatest temptations of my life.

A case of knives
George Herbert

George Herbert (1593–1633) set himself the task of following the ideal of the country parson in the Church of England. He put the conventions of 'metaphysical' poetry to extraordinarily good use. Here he prays to God for deliverance from the afflictions of his soul.

Affliction

Broken in pieces all asunder,
Lord, hunt me not,
A thing forgot,
Once a poor creature, now a wonder,
A wonder tortured in the space
Betwixt this world and that of grace.

My thoughts are all a case of knives,
Wounding my heart
With scattered smart,
As wat'ring pots give flowers their lives.
Nothing their fury can control,
While they do wound and pink my soul.

All my attendants are at strife,
Quitting their place
Unto my face:
Nothing performs the task of life:
The elements are let loose to fight,
And while I live, try out their right.

Oh help, my God! let not their plot
Kill them and me,
And also thee,
Who art my life: dissolve the knot,
As the sun scatters by his light
All the rebellions of the night.

Then shall those powers, which work for grief,
Enter thy pay,
And day by day
Labour thy praise, and my relief;
With care and courage building me,
Till I reach heav'n, and much more, thee.

Leave comfort root-room
Gerard Manley Hopkins

Gerard Manley Hopkins (1844–89) wrote a series of poems known as the 'terrible sonnets' when he was going through a sharp period of desolation or depression. In none of them does he skimp the compression and tautness of his versification. Although there are signs of hope in others of the series, the sonnet below proposes a change of attitude to open himself to the reality of joy.

> My own heart let me more have pity on; let
> Me live to my sad self hereafter kind,
> Charitable; not live this tormented mind
> With this tormented mind tormenting yet.
> I cast for comfort I can no more get
> By groping round my comfortless, than blind
> Eyes in their dark can day or thirst can find
> Thirst's all-in-all in all a world of wet.
> Soul, self; come, poor Jackself, I do advise
> You, jaded, let be; call off thoughts awhile
> Elsewhere; leave comfort root-room; let joy size
> At God knows when to God knows what; whose smile
> 's not wrung, see you; unforeseen times rather – as skies
> Betweenpie mountains – lights a lovely mile.

Shocking vexations
William Law

William Law (1636–1761) changed the lives of John Wesley and Samuel Johnson and John Keble through his book A Serious Call to a Devout and Holy Life *(1729), from which this passage is taken. It approached the serious subject of a Christian life in an often humorous way. Himself debarred from clerical appointments by his refusal to take the oath to George I, Law settled down in Northamptonshire to a regular life of piety and charity, being*

God Almighty has sent us into the world with very few wants; meat, and drink, and cloathing, are the only things necessary in life; and as these are only our present needs, so the present world is well furnish'd to supply these needs.

If a man had half the world in his power, he can make no more of it than this; as he wants it only to supply an animal life, so is it unable to do any thing else for him, or to afford him any other happiness.

This is the state of man, born with few wants, and into a large world very capable of supplying them. So that one would reasonably suppose that men should pass their lives in content and thankfulness to God, at least that they should be free from violent disquiets and vexations, as being placed in a world, that has more than enough to relieve all their wants.

But if to all this we add, that this short life thus furnish'd with all that we want in it is only a short passage to eternal glory, where we shall be cloathed with the brightness of angels, and enter into the joys of God, we might still more reasonably expect, that human life should be a state of peace, and joy, and delight in God. Thus it would certainly be, if reason had its full power over us.

But alas, though God, and Nature, and Reason, make human life thus free from wants, and so full of happiness, yet our passions, in rebellion against God, against Nature and Reason, create a new world of evils, and fill human life with imaginary wants, and vain disquiets.

The man of pride has a thousand wants, which only his own pride has treated; and these render him as full of trouble, as if God had created him with a thousand appetites, without creating any thing that was proper to satisfy them. Envy and Ambition have also their endless wants, which disquiet the souls of men, and by their contradictory motions, render them as foolishly miserable, as those that want to fly and creep at the same time.

Let but any complaining, disquieted man tell you the ground of his uneasiness, and you will plainly see, that he is the author of his own torment; that he is vexing himself at some imaginary evil, which will cease to torment him, as soon as he is content to be that which God, and Nature, and Reason require him to be.

If you should see a man passing his days in disquiet, because he could not walk upon the water, or catch birds as they fly by him, you would readily confess that such a one might thank himself for such uneasiness. But now if you look into all the most tormenting disquiets of life, you will find them all thus absurd; where people are only tormented by their own folly, and vexing themselves at such things as no more concern them, nor are any more their proper good, than walking upon the water, or catching birds.

What can you conceive more silly and extravagant, than to suppose a man racking his brains, and studying night and day how to fly? Wand'ring from his own house and home, wearying himself with climbing upon every ascent, cringing and courting every body he meets, to lift him up from the ground, bruising himself with continual falls, and at last breaking his neck? And all this, from an imagination that it would be glorious to have the eyes of people gazing up at him, and mighty happy to eat, and drink, and sleep, at the top of the highest trees in the kingdom. Would you not readily own, that such a one was only disquieted by his own folly?

If you ask, what it signifies to suppose such silly creatures as these, as are no where to be found in human life?

It may be answer'd, that where-ever you see an ambitious man, there you see this vain and senseless flyer.

Again, if you should see a man that had a large pond of water, yet living in continual thirst, not suffering himself to drink half a draught, for fear of lessening his pond; if you should see him wasting his time and strength, in fetching more water to his pond, always thirsty, yet always carrying a bucket of water in his hand, watching early and late to catch the drops of rain, gaping after every cloud, and running greedily into every mire and mud, in hopes of water, and always studying how to make every ditch empty its self into his pond. If you should see him grow grey and old in these anxious labours, and at last end a careful, thirsty life, by falling into his own pond, would you not say that such a one was not only the author of all his own disquiets, but was foolish enough to be reckon'd amongst ideots and mad men? But yet foolish and absurd as this character is, it does not represent half the follies, and absurd disquiets of the covetous man.

I could now easily proceed to shew the same effects of all our other passions; and make it plainly appear, that all our miseries, vexations, and complaints, are entirely of our own making, and that in the same absurd manner, as in these instances of the covetous and ambitious man. Look where you will, you will see all worldly vexations but like the vexation of him, that was always in mire and mad in search of water to drink, when he had more at home than was sufficient for a hundred horses.

Celia is always telling you how provok'd she is, what intolerable shocking things happen to her, what monstrous usage she suffers, and what vexations she meets with every-where. She tells you that her patience is quite wore out, and there is no bearing the behaviour of people. Every assembly that she is at, sends her home provok'd; something or other has been said, or done, that no reasonable, well bred person ought to bear. Poor people that want her charity, are sent away with hasty answers, not because she has not a heart to part with any money, but because she is too full of some trouble of her own, to attend to the complaints of others. Celia has no business upon her hands, but to receive the income of a plentiful fortune; but yet by the doleful turn of her mind, you would be apt to think, that she had neither food nor lodging.

If you see her look more pale than ordinary, if her lips tremble when she speaks to you, it is because she is just come from a visit, where Lupus took no notice at all of her, but talked all the time to Lucinda, who has not half her fortune. When cross accidents have so disorder'd her spirits, that she is forc'd to send for the Doctor to make her able to eat; she tells him, in great anger at providence, that she never was well since she was born, and that she envies every beggar that she sees in health.

This is the disquiet life of Celia, who has nothing to torment her but her own spirit.

From death to life

The last trial
George MacDonald

George MacDonald (1824–1905) found himself rejected as a Congregational minister by his own congregation. He is certainly a most original thinker, with powers of fantasy that inform his children's fairy-tales and novels for adults. As a religious poet he was admired by Ruskin; C.S. Lewis compiled an anthology of his work. MacDonald did not flinch from dealing with the hardest subjects, and the feeling of abandonment by God that Jesus felt on the cross might at first not seem likely to be a comfort to us. But, as MacDonald says, in it Jesus experienced the deepest trouble a human being can feel. God is with us in our helpless sorrow, and, now, where he has been we can follow.

'My God, my God, why hast thou forsaken me?'
I DO not know that I should dare to approach this, of all utterances into which human breath has ever been moulded, most awful in import, did I not feel that, containing both germ and blossom of the final devotion, it contains therefore the deepest practical lesson the human heart has to learn. The Lord, the Revealer, hides nothing that can be revealed, and will not warn away the foot that treads in naked humility even upon the ground of that terrible conflict between him and Evil, when the smoke of the battle that was fought not only with garments rolled in blood but with burning and fuel of fire, rose up between him and his Father, and for the one terrible moment ere he broke the bonds of life, and walked weary and triumphant into his arms; hid God from the eyes of his Son.

He will give us even to meditate the one thought that slew him at last, when he could bear no more, and fled to the Father to know that he loved him and was well pleased with him. For Satan had come at length yet again, to urge him with his last temptation; to tell him that although he had done his part, God had forgotten his; that although he had lived by the word of his mouth, that mouth had no word more to speak to him; that although he had refused to tempt him, God had left him to be tempted more than he could bear; that although he had worshipped none other, for that worship God did not care. The Lord hides not his sacred sufferings, for truth is light, and would be light in the minds of men. The Holy Child, the Son of the Father, has nothing to conceal, but all the Godhead to reveal. Let us then put off our shoes, and draw near, and bow the head and kiss those feet that bear for ever the scars of our victory. In those feet we clasp the safety of our suffering, our sinning brotherhood.

It is with the holiest fear that we should approach the terrible fact of the sufferings of our Lord. Let no one think that those were less because he was more. The more delicate the nature, the more alive to all that is lovely and true, lawful and right, the more does it feel the antagonism of pain, the inroad of death upon life; the more dreadful is that breach of the harmony of things whose sound is torture. He felt more than man could feel, because he had a larger feeling. He was even therefore worn out sooner than another man would have been. These sufferings were awful indeed when they began to invade the region about the will; when the struggle to keep consciously trusting in God began to sink in darkness; when the Will of The Man put forth its last determined effort in that cry after the vanishing vision of the Father: 'My God, my God, why hast thou forsaken me?' Never had it been so with him before. Never before had he been unable to see God beside him. Yet never was God nearer him than now. For never was Jesus more divine. He could not see, could not feel him near; and yet it is 'My God' that he cries.

Thus the Will of Jesus, in the very moment when his faith seems about to yield, is finally triumphant. It has no feeling now to support it, no beatific vision to absorb it. It stands naked in his soul and tortured, as he stood naked and scourged before Pilate. Pure and simple and surrounded by fire, it declares for God. The sacrifice ascends in the cry, 'My God'. The cry comes not out of happiness, out of peace, out of hope. Not even out of suffering comes that cry. It was a cry in

65

desolation, but it came out of Faith. It is the last voice of Truth, speaking when it can but cry. The divine horror of that moment is unfathomable by human soul. It was blackness of darkness. And yet he would believe. Yet he would hold fast. God was his God yet. 'My God' – and in the cry came forth the Victory, and all was over soon. Of the peace that followed that cry, the peace of a perfect soul, large as the universe, pure as light, ardent as life, victorious for God and his brethren, he himself alone can ever know the breadth and length, and depth and height.

Without this last trial of all, the temptations of our Master had not been so full as the human cup could hold; there would have been one region through which we had to pass wherein we might call aloud upon our Captain-Brother, and there would be no voice or hearing: he had avoided the fatal spot! The temptations of the desert came to the young, strong man with his road before him and the presence of his God around him; nay, gathered their very force from the exuberance of his conscious faith. 'Dare and do, for God is with thee,' said the devil. 'I know it, and therefore I will wait,' returned the king of his brothers.

And now, after three years of divine action, when his course is run, when the old age of finished work is come, when the whole frame is tortured until the regnant brain falls whirling down the blue gulf of fainting, and the giving up of the ghost is at hand, when the friends have forsaken him and fled, comes the voice of the enemy again at his ear: 'Despair and die, for God is not with thee. All is in vain. Death, not Life, is thy refuge. Make haste to Hades, where thy torture will be over. Thou hast deceived thyself. He never was with thee. He was the God of Abraham. Abraham is dead. Whom makest thou thyself?' 'My God, my God, why hast thou forsaken me?' the Master cries. For God was his God still, although he had forsaken him – forsaken his vision that his faith might glow out triumphant. Forsaken himself? No; come nearer to him than ever; come nearer, even as – but with a yet deeper, more awful pregnancy of import – even as the Lord himself withdrew from the bodily eyes of his friends, that he might dwell in their profoundest being.

I do not think it was our Lord's deepest trial when in the garden he prayed that the cup might pass from him, and prayed yet again that the will of the Father might be done. For that Will was then present with him. He was living and acting in that Will. But now the foreseen horror has come. He is drinking the dread cup, and the Will has vanished from his eyes. Were that Will visible in his suffering, his will could bow with tearful gladness under the shelter of its grandeur. But now his Will is left alone to drink the cup of The Will in torture. In the sickness of this agony, the Will of Jesus arises perfect at last; and of itself, unsupported now, declares – a naked consciousness of misery hung in the waste darkness of the universe – declares for God, in defiance of pain, of death, of apathy, of self, of negation, of the blackness within and around it; calls aloud upon the vanished God.

This is the Faith of the Son of God. God withdrew, as it were, that the perfect Will of the Son might arise and go forth to find the Will of the Father.

Is it possible that even then he thought of the lost sheep who could not believe that God was their Father; and for them, too, in all their loss and blindness and unlove, cried, saying the word they might say, knowing for them that God means Father and more, and knowing now, as he had never known till now, what a fearful thing it is to be without God and without hope? I dare not answer the question I put.

But wherein or what can this Alpine apex of faith have to do with the creatures who call themselves Christians, creeping about in the valleys, hardly knowing that there are mountains above them, save that they take offence at and stumble over the pebbles washed across their path by the glacier streams? I will tell you. We are and remain such creeping Christians, because we look at ourselves and not at Christ; because we gaze at the marks of our own soiled feet, and the trail of our own defiled garments, instead of up at the snows of purity, whither the soul of Christ clomb. Each, putting his foot in the footprint of the Master, and so defacing it, turns to examine how far his neighbour's footprint corresponds with that which he still calls the Master's, although it is but his own. Or, having committed a petty fault, I mean a fault such as only a petty creature could commit, we mourn over the defilement to ourselves, and the shame of it before our friends, children, or servants, instead of hastening to make the due confession and amends to our fellow, and then, forgetting our paltry self with its well-earned disgrace, lift up our eyes to the glory which alone will quicken the true man in us, and kill the piddling creature we so wrongly call our self. The true self is that which can look Jesus in the face, and say 'My Lord'.

When the inward sun is shining, and the wind of thought, blowing where it lists amid the flowers and leaves of fancy and imagination, rouses glad forms and feelings, it is easy to look upwards, and say 'My God'. It is easy when the frosts of external failure have braced the mental nerves to healthy endurance and fresh effort after labour; it is easy then to turn to God and trust in him, in whom all honest exertion gives an ability as well as a right to trust. It is easy in pain, so long as it does not pass certain undefinable bounds; to hope in God for deliverance, or pray for strength to endure. But what is to be done when all feeling is gone? When a man does not know whether he believes or not, whether he loves or not? When art, poetry, religion are nothing to him, so swallowed up is he in pain, or mental depression, or disappointment, or temptation, or he knows not what? It seems to him then that God does not care for him, and certainly he does not care for God. If he is still humble, he thinks that he is so bad that God cannot care for him. And he then believes for the time that God loves us only because and when and while we love him; instead of believing that God loves us always because he is our God, and that we live only by his love. Or he does not believe in a God at all, which is better.

So long as we have nothing to say to God, nothing to do with him, save in the sunshine of the mind when we feel him near us, we are poor creatures, willed upon, not willing, reeds, flowering reeds, it may be, and pleasant to behold, but only reeds blown about of the wind; not bad, but poor creatures.

And how in such a condition do we generally act? Do we not sit mourning over the loss of our feelings? Or worse, make frantic efforts to rouse them? Or, ten times worse, relapse into a state of temporary atheism, and yield to the pressing temptation? Or, being heartless, consent to remain careless, conscious of evil thoughts and low feelings alone, but too lazy, too content to rouse ourselves against them? We know we must get rid of them some day, but meantime – never mind; we do not feel them bad, we do not feel anything else good; we are asleep and we know it, and we cannot be troubled to wake. No impulse comes to arouse us, and so we remain as we are.

God does not, by the instant gift of his Spirit, make us always feel right, desire good, love purity, aspire after him and his Will. Therefore either he will not, or he cannot. If he will not, it must be because it would not be well to do so. If he cannot, then he would not if he could; else a better condition than God's is conceivable to the mind of God – a condition in which he could save the creatures whom he has made, better than he can save them. The truth is this: he wants to make us in his own image, choosing the good, refusing the evil. How should he effect this if he were always moving us from within, as he does at divine intervals, towards the beauty of holiness? God gives us room to be; does not oppress us with his will; 'stands away from us', that we may act from ourselves, that we may exercise the pure will for good. Do not, therefore, imagine me to mean that we can do anything of ourselves without God. If we choose the right at last, it is all God's doing, and only the more his that it is ours, only in a far more marvellous way his than if he had kept us filled with all holy impulses precluding the need of choice. For up to this very point, or this very point, he has been educating us, leading us, pushing us, driving us, enticing us, that we may choose him and his Will, and so be tenfold more his children, of his own best making, in the freedom of the Will found our own first in its loving sacrifice to him, for which in his grand fatherhood he has been thus working from the foundations of the earth, than we could be in the most ecstatic worship flowing from the divinest impulse, without this willing sacrifice. For God made our individuality as well as, and a greater marvel than, our dependence; made our apartness from himself, that freedom should bind us divinely dearer to himself, with a new and inscrutable marvel of love; for the Godhead is still at the root, is the making root of our individuality, and the freer the man, the stronger the bond that binds him to him who made his freedom.

He made our wills, and is striving to make them free; for only in the perfection of our individuality and the freedom of our wills can we be altogether his children. This is full of mystery, but can we not see enough in it to make us very glad and very peaceful?

Not in any other act than one which, in spite of impulse or of weakness, declares for the Truth, for God, does the Will spring into absolute freedom, into true life.

See, then, what lies within our reach every time that we are thus lapt in the folds of night. The highest condition of the human Will is in sight, is attainable. I say not the highest condition of the Human Being; that surely lies in the Beatific Vision, in the sight of God. But the highest condition of the Human Will, as distinct, not as separated from God, is when, not seeing God, not seeming to itself to grasp him at all, it yet holds him fast. It cannot continue in this condition, for, not finding, not seeing God, the man would die; but the Will thus asserting itself, the man has passed from death into life, and the vision is nigh at hand. Then first, thus free, in thus asserting its freedom, is the individual will one with the Will of God; the child is finally restored to the father; the childhood and the fatherhood meet in one; the brotherhood of the race arises from the dust; and the prayer of our Lord is answered, 'I in them and thou in me, that they may be made perfect in one.' Let us then arise in God-born strength every time that we feel the darkness closing, or become aware that it has closed around us, and say, 'I am of the Light and not of the Darkness.'

Troubled soul, thou art not bound to feel, but thou art bound to arise. God loves thee whether thou feelest or not. Thou canst not love when thou wilt, but thou art bound to fight the hatred in thee to the last. Try not to feel good when thou art not good, but cry to Him who is good. He changes not because thou changest. Nay, he has an especial tenderness of love towards thee for that thou art in the dark and hast no light, and his heart is glad when thou dost arise and say, 'I will go to my Father.' For he sees thee through all the gloom through which thou canst not see him. Will thou his Will. Say, to him: 'My God, I am very dull and low and hard; but thou art wise and high and tender, and thou art my God. I am thy child. Forsake me not.' Then fold the arms of thy faith, and wait in quietness until light goes up in thy darkness. Fold the arms of thy Faith I say, but not of thy Action: bethink thee of something that thou oughtest to do, and go and do it, if it be but the sweeping of a room, or the preparing of a meal, or a visit to a friend. Heed not thy feelings: Do thy work.

As God lives by his own will, and we live in him, so has he given to us power to will in ourselves. How much better should we not fare if, finding that we are standing with our heads bowed away from the good, finding that we have no feeble inclination to seek the source of our life, we should yet will upwards toward God, rousing that essence of life in us, which he has given us from his own heart, to call again upon him who is our Life, who can fill the emptiest heart, rouse the deadest conscience, quicken the dullest feeling, and strengthen the feeblest will.

Then, if ever the time should come, as perhaps it must come to each of us, when all consciousness of well-being shall have vanished, when the earth shall be but a sterile promontory, and the heavens a dull and pestilent congregation of vapours, when man nor woman shall delight us more, nay, when God himself shall be but a name, and Jesus an old story, then, even then, when a Death far worse than 'that phantom of grisly bone' is griping at our hearts, and having slain love, hope, faith, forces existence upon us only in agony, then, even then, we shall be able to cry out with our Lord, 'My God, my God, why hast thou forsaken me?' Nor shall we die then, I think, without being able to take up his last words as well, and say, 'Father, into thy hands I commend my spirit.'

71

Jaws of the fish
Bede

Bede (673–735) wrote a commentary on the biblical book of Tobit in what seems to us a surprising fashion. The cheerful story of young Tobias involves, to be sure, the vanquishing of the devil. Bede eagerly applies the events of the story to the actions of Jesus in the New Testament. In this passage he explains that Jesus did not greatly fear the devil, but, as man, did fear death, which the devil had brought into the world; and yet Jesus freely underwent death to wash us free from its contagion.

6:1–2

Having set out with the angel as guide, Tobias paused by the river Tigris for the first break in his journey, and went out to wash his feet, and, lo and behold, a huge fish came up to devour him. Here again the mystery of the Lord's Passion is quite obviously signified. For the huge fish, which, since he wanted to devour him, was killed by Tobias on the angel's instructions, represents the ancient devourer of the human race – the devil. When the latter desired the death of humanity in our Redeemer, he was caught by the power of the divinity.

The river Tigris which, because of its swift current, takes its name from the tiger, a very swift animal, intimates the downward course of our death and mortality. In it lurked a huge fish inasmuch as the invisible seducer of the human race held the power of death. Tobias stopped over by the waters of the Tigris because the Lord, when he appeared in the world, spent his life among sinners and mortals; but the water of sin did not touch him, nor did the prince of darkness, when he came, find in him anything of his own. On the other hand, Tobias went out into the river to wash his feet; and the Lord embraced death to which he was under no obligation, in order to wash all the faithful, his members, free from the contagion of sin and death. The fish rushed at Tobias eager to devour him; and when the Lord had suffered on the cross, the devil, who had ordered him to be crucified, came to see if perhaps he could find any sin in his soul.

6:3

Tobias being very frightened of the fish shouted aloud saying: Sir, he is coming at me. And the Lord as the critical moment of death was upon him began to tremble with fear and be deeply dismayed, not that he was greatly afraid of the devil but, through the natural frailty of the flesh, dreaded death which entered the world through the devil's envy. This is why he also prayed that, if it were possible, the hour might pass from him, and said: 'Abba, Father, all things are possible to you; remove this cup from me, but not what I will but what you will.'

6:4

The angel said to Tobias: Take the fish by the gill and pull him towards you. The Lord seized hold of the devil and by dying caught and conquered the one who wanted to catch him in death. Moreover he seized him by the gill so that, with the right hand of his power, he might separate his most wicked head from his entrapped body, that is, that he might remove the wickedness of the ancient enemy from the heart of those whom he had wickedly allied to himself and had made, as it were, one body with him, and that, as a merciful redeemer, he might graft them into the body of his Church. For a fish has a gill at the joining of its head and body. Now, just as our Lord is the head of his Church and the Church is his body, so the devil is the head of all the wicked and all the wicked are his head and members. The reason why the Lord seized the very savage fish by the gill, dragged it towards him and cast it up on dry land was that, in smashing them to pieces, he openly and boldly exposed the devil's capabilities in public, and rescued from the power of darkness those whom he foreknew to be children of light.

Buried with Christ
Ronald Knox

*Ronald Knox (1888–1955) was a priest who made money from writing
witty books and newspaper articles in order to subsidize his work of biblical
scholarship and spiritual counselling. Here, in an extract from his book*
St Paul's Gospel *(1953) he explores the idea of dying with Christ in Baptism
and thus living a new life in grace, no longer the frustated slaves of the law. The
figure of the ark which Knox, as it were, floats, is discussed by Hugh of
St Victor on a later page.*

St Paul is very fond of the word 'completion', and it may be true that
he was using, in an orthodox sense, the language of those heretics
whose false teaching was a danger to the Church at Colossae. But I
sometimes wonder whether it may not have suggested to him,
besides, a familiar image.

St Paul came from Tarsus, a place of ships and seamen; less than a
century before, it had been the great centre of piracy in the Mediter-
ranean. And the Greeks talked about 'completing' a ship where we
should talk of 'manning' a ship; described the crew of a ship as its
'completion'. Did he, perhaps, at the back of his mind, think of the
Sacred Humanity as a ship, an ark, which would have meant nothing if there had been no crew to sail it?

On the other side, hard as it may be to think of ourselves as the
completing of Christ's nature, there is no difficulty whatever in realizing that he is the completion of ours. 'In Christ,' says the Apostle,
'the whole plenitude of Deity is embodied, and in him you find your
completion ... You, by baptism, have been united to his burial,
united, too, with his resurrection' (Colossians 2:10). Man's nature,
ever since the Fall, incapable of achieving his clear destiny, conscious, however dimly, of the desire to please God, yet with no apparatus for doing it – how could anything be so manifestly incomplete?

Compare him, if you will, to a ship bound for some distant port,
with no complement of sailors to man her. You would almost expect
to find St Paul comparing Christian baptism with the rescue of

Noe and his sons in the ark. But he doesn't; it is St Peter who does that (First Epistle of Peter 3:20). For St Paul, the type of baptism is the people of Israel, led out from its Egyptian bondage through the Red Sea.

That analogy will have been in the minds of Christian people from the first; it could hardly be otherwise. Our Lord suffered death at the time of the great Jewish feast; evidently he meant us to understand that he was being sacrificed for us as our Paschal Victim, meant us to understand that the escape of Israel from Egypt by way of the Red Sea was a type of Christian baptism, cutting us off, as if by a wall of water, from our dead past. The hymn Exsultet, which we sing on Holy Saturday, a hymn that in its whole inspiration takes you right back to the very beginnings of Christendom, is full of that imagery. 'This night, long ago, thou didst rescue the sons of Israel, our fathers, out of Egypt, over the Red Sea bidding them pass dry-shod; none but this, with pillar of cloud to enlighten it, shadow of man's sin could purge away.' So we bless the candle that is the type of our Lord himself, that will be dipped into the new Font, and make it pregnant with the power of spiritual re-birth. All that, or at least the doctrinal kernel of all that, St Paul knew about; we learn as much from a casual reference, a single word of one of his letters – how prodigal he is of unexploited allusion, throwing out a significant word to us, and passing on!

He is warning the Corinthians that it is a fatal error to presume on one's grace; you must co-operate with it energetically; he who thinks he stands firmly should beware of a fall. And he illustrates that by recalling the infidelities of the Jewish people in the wilderness; they (he says) could sin and did sin in spite of the great graces bestowed on them. Had they not been saved from the pursuit of their enemies by the cloud that overhung their camp, by the waters of the Red Sea which closed behind them? Only he does not use that phrase, 'Saved from the pursuit of their enemies'; his words are, 'All alike, in the cloud and in the sea, were baptized into Moses' fellowship' (First Epistle to the Corinthians, 10:2). What he means, evidently, is that Christian baptism, intimately connected with our

Lord's Resurrection and with the feast of our Lord's Resurrection, is the fulfilment of a type; it puts a distance between us and our sins, isolates us in the close unity of Christian fellowship; we too are like men who have escaped from bondage, rallied now under divine leadership. On all that background of his thought the Apostle just lifts, as it were, the corner of a curtain when, almost absentmindedly, he calls the crossing of the Red Sea a baptism.

But of course, from his point of view, the type is only a feeble image, it doesn't do justice to the situation. The Israelites, when they escaped from Egypt, escaped with their lives; it is not so with Christian baptism. To be baptized is to undergo a mystical death, in union with our Lord's death on the cross, a mystical burial in union with his burial, a mystical resurrection in union with his resurrection. We have been taken up into Christ's death, 'in our baptism, we have been buried with him, died like him, that so, just as Christ was raised up by his Father's power from the dead, we too might live and move in a new kind of existence'. We are grafted into a new stock; 'our former nature has been crucified with him, and the living power of our guilt destroyed, so that we are the slaves of sin no longer. Guilt makes no more claim on a man who is dead' (Romans 6:6).

Do not ask St Paul whether this mystical death sets us free from the old law, or sets us free from guilt; it is the same process – the burden we carried when we were still unregenerate was that of an obligation we could not meet; the law and our sinfulness played into one another's hands, were the upper and nether millstone which ground us between them. Now it is all right; we are dead, and death cancels all obligations. Elsewhere, pressing his imagery still more boldly, he tells us that we are dead, and our life is hidden away with Christ in God (Colossians 3:3); we take refuge from our pursuers, and our hiding-place is a tomb.

Not that St Paul is unacquainted with that other and more familiar imagery which describes baptism as washing us clean from our sins; 'He saved us with the cleaning power which gives us new birth' (Titus 3:5). But that is not his favourite way of talking; and,

I think, for two reasons. Washing is something external to ourselves, we get rid of something on the surface that was never really part of us, whereas the grace of baptism goes down to the very roots of our nature, restores us to a new kind of existence. And washing is a process we may repeat as often as we will; baptism is not like that, it is a single, crucial moment like the moment of death.

Dead, buried, and risen with Christ, that is our state, when we have been baptized. We must not imagine, when St Paul uses a legal metaphor about death cancelling all claims, that he looks on this baptism-death as a mere legal fiction. No, we must think of ourselves as dead to sin, and alive with a life that looks towards God (Romans 6:11). New life, for St Paul, does not mean merely new habits of living, turning over a new leaf. It means that a new principle of life altogether has been implanted in us; it is as if God were repeating that act by which he breathed life into the dumb clay of his creature Adam, long ago in Paradise.

There are passages in which you will find the Apostle pressing this notion still further, as if the change which takes place in us at baptism were something more, even, than a death and a rising again; as if it involved the annihilation of the thing we once were, and the creation of a fresh human being altogether. 'Circumcision means nothing,' he tells the Galatians, 'and the want of it means nothing; when a man is in Christ Jesus, there has been a new creation' (Galatians, 6:15). And so, in a passage I have already quoted, he insists that our old self has been crucified with Christ (Romans 6:6).

Of course, by a metaphor, you may talk of a man's old self and his new self when he has undergone any considerable change of heart. But St Paul seems to mean more than that; does he mean (we are tempted to ask) that the regeneration which comes to us with baptism undoes all the effects of the Fall, that we no longer feel the sting of concupiscence, that we are sealed, irresistibly and automatically, for heaven? But no, that is not what he is telling us. On the contrary, in these very passages where he insists so strongly on the catastrophic effects of the new birth, he is pleading with us to live up to it and be worthy of it. 'You must be quit, now, of the old self whose

77

way of life you remember, the self that wasted its aim on false dreams. ... You must be quit of the old self, and the habits that went with it; you must be clothed in the new self, that is being refitted all the time for closer knowledge, so that the image of the God who created it is its pattern' (Ephesians 6:22; Colossians 3:9). He tells us that we have got to get rid of the old self, not that we are rid of it. The doctrine of the new birth is not an All-clear signal to tell us that the struggle with sin is all over. It is a call to arms, bidding us enter on the struggle, because at last we have a chance of victory. 'You must not make your bodily powers over to sin. ... Sin will not be able to play the master over you any longer; you serve grace now, not the law' (Romans 6:13).

You serve grace now, not the law – that means, evidently and most importantly, a better chance in the struggle, the law does but set before us a high standard, which we despair of achieving, grace enables us. But something else, I think, is implied. When you serve the law, you serve it, inevitably, in a legal spirit, unwillingly, grudgingly, according to the letter. When you serve free grace, you serve it in a spirit of freedom; you enter (as we say) into the spirit of it, co-operate, gladly and generously, with its designs for you. That contrast between doing God's will because you have got to and doing God's will because you want to is more explicitly set forth elsewhere. When the Jews were rescued from their bondage in Egypt, they emerged (you might almost say) from one bondage into another; they were God's slaves now instead of Pharaoh's, obeying him, if they obeyed him at all, blindly, unquestioningly, as they obeyed Pharaoh. But when the grace of Jesus Christ came to us, it was no longer, this time, a mere change of masters. 'The spirit you have now received is not, as of old, a spirit of slavery, to govern you by fear; it is the spirit of adoption, which makes us cry out Abba, Father!' (Romans 8:15).

It is the same principle which our Lord himself had taught, though with a slightly different emphasis, when he told his Apostles, 'I do not speak of you now as my servants; a servant is one who does not understand what his master is about, whereas I have made known to you all that my Father has told me, and so I have called you my friends' (John 15:15). If the practice of the Christian religion seems to you and me something uncommonly like drudgery, that is our fault; it was not meant to be. The only really Christian attitude is to obey God with the dutifulness of loving sons, is to follow Christ with the loyalty of devoted friends.

Two styles of dying

Cardinal Wiseman
John Morris

An extraordinary account of the highest Victorian deathbed scene is given by John Morris, the secretary of Cardinal Wiseman, in his curious little book The Last Illness of His Eminence Cardinal Wiseman *(1865).*

Wiseman had been Archbishop of Westminster for more than 14 years when he was taken ill with blistering of his right foot. He had been diabetic since 1853, and although his foot healed, by January 12 he was afflicted with erysipelas. This is now known to be a streptococcal infection. For Wiseman the only alleviation of the painful swelling around one eye was the constant bathing with icy water performed by the Reverend Mother who attended him as nurse. A surgeon periodically cut into carbuncles that developed.

The striking element in Morris's narrative is the contrast between the formal insistence by Wiseman on all the pomps of church ceremony and his genuine quiet fortitude in suffering a month's painful dying while retaining a friendly informality with his carers.

Wiseman seemed almost to identify the Church with external ceremonies. 'I never cared for anything,' he said, 'but the Church. My sole delight has been everything connected with her. As people in the world would go to a ball for their recreation, so I have enjoyed a great function.' He had his bed moved downstairs to a room big enough to hold the assembled canons of the cathedral gathered round him for the ceremonies consigning him on his last journey.

But he showed no frustration when he grew unable to swallow and so receive the Sacrament of Communion that he craved. And all the while he joked with Morris and the nun looking after him.

When the doctors had left him, and Reverend Mother had returned, he said to her, 'Well, did you hear what they said?' She answered, 'No, father; but I can guess.' 'They tell me I am going home. Is it not nice?' 'For you,' she said, 'but not for us.' 'Oh, it is so nice: it is like going home for the holidays after working hard at school. Do not you know the feeling of going home? I am going to be with my Father. I am going to rest; – no more work, no more troubles, no more scoldings, all peace. I am just like a child going home to rest and be with its Father.' . . .

'I do not wish any one to read to me when I am dying,' he said, 'but I had rather be left to my own meditations.' I remarked, 'But you would like to have the Litany, my lord?' 'What, the Commendation of a Departing Soul, the Church's words,' he answered, quite brightening up. 'I want to have every thing the Church gives me, down to the Holy Water. Do not leave out any thing. I want every thing.'

He was vested, as he lay in bed, by Monsignor Searle, who had so often vested him before. He had on his rochet, his red mozzetta and zucchetto, his pectoral cross and gold stele; and he wore the sapphire ring which, when he was made a Cardinal, he received from the College of the Propaganda, in return for the offering which it is their privilege to receive from all newly-created members of the Sacred College. I said to him, 'Canon Hunt, as the Missionary Rector will anoint your Eminence.' He bowed his head. I added, 'And will you have the Asperges from the Senior Canon?' He answered, looking round at me, 'I want every thing.'

The Canons then came into the room, wearing their choir dress, and formed a semicircle around him, on his left side. Mr Patterson was there, as his Master of Ceremonies. He had previously requested Monsignor Searle to assist him on his right hand; and he told me to be on his left, and to read the Profession of Faith for him. The large picture of Pope Pius IX, which all who have been in his drawing room will remember, looked down upon us, and seemed to form part of the group, who were engaged in one of the most solemn acts the Church has devised. The Archiepiscopal Cross was placed at the foot of the bed; and there it remained for the days of his life that were yet left.

Canon Maguire, as the Senior Canon, in the absence of the Provost, having sprinkled the Cardinal with holy water, I knelt by his

81

side and read the Creed of Pope Pius IV. When it was ended, the book of the Gospels was handed to him to kiss, for the oath with which it concludes. He put his hand upon it, and said, 'Put it down.' And then, 'I wish to express before the Chapter that I have not, and never have had in my whole life, the very slightest doubt or hesitation of any one of the Articles of this Faith; I have always endeavoured to teach it; and I transmit it intact to my successor.'

The Missal was then lifted up to him, and he kissed it, saying, 'Sic me Deus adjuvet et haec Sancta Dei Evangelia.' He then added, 'I now wish to receive Extreme Unction at your hands, as the seal of my Profession of Faith.'

That same Sunday evening another painful operation was requisite. For some time before he left his bedroom, a large carbuncle had formed on the right temple. Mr Hawkins had tried, if possible, to prevent its growth by burning it with caustic; but the use of the knife became necessary; and in the evening, after he had received the Chapter, it was opened with three cross cuts, in the form of a star. There had been two cuts in each former operation, the third was therefore unexpected, but he only very slightly winced. Dangerous as it was, the knife passing the arteries of the temple within the distance of the thickness of the paper on which I write, and though he was so weak that not a drop of blood could be spared, the operation was quite necessary, as the doctors said, in order 'to give him a chance'. To Mr Hawkins he said, 'What you think it right to do, it is my duty to submit to. Remember that.' His remark to the medical man, when the time came, was 'I am in your hands; do with me as you like.'

In the night after this operation, the Cardinal called Reverend Mother to him, and said, 'How do I come to be here?' She thought he meant in that room, and answered, 'You came down on Friday.' 'I mean how do I come to be here? They promised me I should be in heaven to-night.' She said, 'They are trying to keep you with us a little longer. It is very selfish, but we want you a little longer.' And then he said very low, as if he did not wish any one to hear, 'Do you know I could not help thinking, while they were cutting me, that it was very unkind to try to keep me out of Heaven. I had been hoping all day that I should go home to-night.' Afterwards he said, 'Will this make me well?' Reverend Mother answered that it was the only chance. 'If I do recover at all, shall I be fit for work? Because if not, I shall be only in the way.' She said that she supposed that if he got better he would be fit for work, but not for a long time. 'I do not think I shall get better. I feel my strength going out of me, and nothing does me any good.' And then he said something about being disappointed, but that he must have patience. 'Pray that I may be patient.'

I asked him, 'Are you always thinking of God?' He answered, 'Oh, of course!'

A little later in the evening he was moved into his chair, and Reverend Mother was bathing his eye, while I was kneeling by him. He made an effort to tell us his meditation on heaven, but he was tired, and the right words would not come. He said, 'Do not think I am wandering, for I am not.' And he was not, but only some sentences were audible, and it was clear that his memory did not serve him with the words that would express his thoughts. I heard some such sentences as 'diamonds, and on every facet a Virgin or a Martyr'. And then the two striking phrases, 'Rush through the angels into God'; and after a time, during which he had evidently been pondering on the eternity of the Beatific Vision, 'I never heard of any one being tired of the stars.' . . .

At eight o'clock in the morning of Wednesday the 15th of February, with the Church's words sounding in his ears, as he had desired, he passed away to his rest.

Francis of Assisi
Thomas of Celano

Thomas of Celano (1200–55) knew Francis of Assisi (1182–1226) and wrote two biographies of him, the second of which, from which the passage below is taken, was completed about 20 years after Francis's death. Francis had been

very sick for two years, his body weak and his eyesight sometimes disappearing.
The reference in Thomas's account here to his hiding with his hand the wound
on his side concerns the stigmata or marks of Jesus's crucifixion, the wounds
in the hands, feet and side, that Francis was granted miraculously but about
which he remained humbly reticent. To the end Francis remained aware of his
position as a teacher and father of his brothers and of his own utter poverty and
reliance on God.

Worn down by his serious illness that was being brought to an
end with every suffering, he had himself placed naked upon the
naked ground, so that in that final hour when the enemy could
still rage against him, he might wrestle naked with a naked enemy.
He waited without fear for his triumph, and with his hands clasped
he was grasping a crown of justice.

Placed thus upon the ground, with his garment of sackcloth
laid aside, he raised his face to heaven as was his custom, and giving
his whole attention to that glory, he covered the wound in his right
side with his left hand lest it be seen. And he said to his brothers:
'I have done what was mine to do; may Christ teach you what you
are to do.'

Seeing these things his sons shed streams of tears and sighing
deeply from their innermost being, they were overwhelmed by
grief in their compassion. Meanwhile, when their sighs were somewhat quieted, Francis's guardian, who knew the saint's wish more
exactly by reason of divine inspiration, hurriedly arose and taking
a tunic and trousers and a little cap of sackcloth, he said to their
father: 'Know that this tunic and trousers and cap have been lent
to you by me, by command of holy obedience. But, that you may
know that you have no ownership with regard to them, I take away
from you all authority to give them to anyone.' The saint rejoiced
and was glad out of the gladness of his heart, for he saw that he
had kept faith with Lady Poverty to the end! For he had done
all these things out of zeal for poverty, so that he would not have
at the end even a habit that was his own, but, as it were, lent to
him by another.

After these things, the saint raised his hands to heaven and praised his Christ, because, freed now of all things, he was going to him free. Indeed, that he might show himself to be a true imitator of Christ his God in all things, he loved to the end his brothers and sons whom he had loved from the beginning. He had all the brothers present there called to him and soothing them with comforting words in view of his death, he exhorted them with paternal affection to love God. He spoke a long time about practising patience and poverty, setting the counsels of the holy Gospel ahead of all other prescriptions. Then, with all the brothers sitting about, he extended his right hand over them and beginning with his vicar, he placed it upon the head of each one.

While therefore the brothers were weeping very bitterly and grieving inconsolably, the holy father commanded that bread be brought to him. He blessed and broke it and gave a small piece of it to each one to eat. Commanding also that a book of the Gospels be brought, he asked that the Gospel according to St John be read to him from the place that begins: Before the feast of the Passover. He was recalling that most holy supper which the Lord celebrated as his last supper with his disciples. He did all of this in reverent memory of that supper, showing thereby the deep love he had for his brothers.

Then he spent the few days that remained before his death in praise, teaching his companions whom he loved so much to praise Christ with him. He himself, in as far as he was able, broke forth in this psalm: 'I cried to the Lord with my voice: with my voice I made supplication to the Lord.' He also invited all creatures to praise God, and by means of the words he had composed earlier, he exhorted them to love God. He exhorted death itself, terrible and hateful to all, to give praise, and going joyfully to meet it, he invited it to make its lodging with him. 'Welcome,' he said, 'my sister death.'

To the doctor he said: 'Tell me bravely, brother doctor, that death, which is the gateway of life, is at hand.'

Then to the brothers: 'When you see that I am brought to my last moments, place me naked upon the ground just as you saw me the day before yesterday; and let me lie there after I am dead for the length of time it takes one to walk a mile unhurriedly.' The hour therefore came, and all the mysteries of Christ being fulfilled in him, he winged his way happily to God.

Surviving others

I will not let him go
Edward Bouverie Pusey

Edward Bouverie Pusey (1800–82) was Regius Professor of Hebrew at Oxford and a Canon of Christ Church from 1828 till his death. Newman joined him in the Oxford Movement to renew sacramental and devotional life in the Church of England. Pusey defended the Real Presence of Jesus in the Eucharist and helped found an Anglican convent. Unlike others in the Oxford Movement he remained in the Church of England. He entitled the sermon from which the passage below is taken 'Joy out of suffering', but he knew that the book of Job in the Bible wrestles long and hard with the mystery of suffering. His thoughts connect with those of George MacDonald, above.

'Though He slay me, yet will I trust Him' – Job 13:15
We must not, would not, choose our suffering. 'Any pang but this,' is too often the wounded spirit's cry; 'any trouble but this.' And its cry may bear witness to itself, that its Merciful Physician knows well where its disease lies, how it is to be probed to the quick, how to be healthfully healed. 'Though He slay me, yet will I trust in Him.' The holy Patriarch says not, 'though He slay all my children at one blow', 'though He send His sore judgments of fire and sword, and take away my goods', 'though He strip me naked, as I came from my mother's womb, and make me sit down in ashes', 'though He smite me from head to foot with sores, and put my brethren far from me, and I become strange to my wife, and young children despise me'; – for all this, and more, had God already done. He saith, 'though He slay me'.

This great servant of God takes, unknowing, into his mouth, the very words wherewith Satan had slandered him. 'Skin for skin,' said the Accuser, 'yea, all that a man hath, will he give in exchange for his life.' As if he would say, 'He bears what moves him less, for fear of what would touch him nearer; he hopes that suffering without may save him from sufferings within; he gives willingly that he hath to save that he is: his patience is a subtle love of self; he bears not all this for love of Thee, or out of faith in Thee and hope in Thee, but out of love for self, and the hope to escape what may wound self most deeply. Let the iron enter into his soul, and he will deny Thee then.'

And Job, though he knew it not, was given over into the Accuser's hands. All he might destroy, except that inner life, whereby he held fast to God. 'Behold he is in thine hand; but save his life.' For how should Satan touch that life, which is God's very Presence in the soul? And Job, in those great words, refutes Satan's lie, 'Though He slay me, yet will I trust in Him.' He holds not back his very self. He gives up freely all which he is, his very I; like that devout Christian soul which, when sore pressed and oppressed by heaviness, yet held him fast by God, and said in an ecstasy of love and trust, 'If God casts me into Hell, I will hold so fast by Him, that He shall go there too; I will not let Him go, and Hell will be no Hell to me.' Truly! – for the love of God would make Hell Heaven, as its absence would make Heaven Hell.

'Though He slay me'? Oh glorious faith of older Saints, and hope of the Resurrection, and love stronger than death, and blessed bareness of the soul, which, for God, would part with all but God, knowing that in God it will find all; yea, which would give its very self, trusting Him Who took itself from itself, that it should find again, (as all the redeemed will find,) itself a better self in God!

'Though He slay me, yet will I trust in Him.' Oh blessed passage of the soul through the valley of death, which dies, to live; which hopes, though in a way she is not; which is and is not; is slain and trusteth in Him Who slayeth her; 'dieth, and behold she lives'. For the soul lives, not in herself, but 'by the faith in the Son of God, Who loved her, and gave Himself for her'. Not she lives, but 'He liveth in her'; and so death to all but Him, yea, to and in her very self also, is His enlarged Life to her. It is the very life of the Blessed, to be nothing in themselves, but vessels wherein God can pour in the fullness,

and bliss, and richness, and transporting, overpowering, overwhelming sweetness and tenderness of His Love, and they, not of
themselves, but through and with His Own Love, shall love Himself.
It is the very Joy of their Lord, whereinto they shall enter, to joy not
with their own joy, but with His; to be themselves, only to be not
themselves; to be, only to have them the Being of God, Which is
His Love.

An end to grieving
Alcuin

*Alcuin (735–804) was an Englishman, but wrote this piece of verse in Latin, a
language through which he communicated with all Europe in his time. Helen
Waddell, on translating it, remarked that it probably came originally at the
end of a letter.*

> Come, make an end of singing and of grieving,
> But not an end of love.
> I wrote this song, beloved, bitter weeping,
> And yet I know 'twill prove
> That by God's grace,
> We two shall see each other face to face,
> And stand together with a heart at rest.

Where is God?
C.S. Lewis

*C.S. Lewis (1898–1963) was an Oxford don specializing in Renaissance stu-
dies;* The Discarded Image, *on medieval cosmology, and* A Preface to
Paradise Lost, *really a study of the epic, are among his shorter works of enduring excellence. He was converted to Christianity after many years of unbelief
and is universally known today as a children's author and writer on spiritual*

matters. In 1952 he met Joy Davidman, whom he married in 1956. She died, aged 45, in 1960. In 1961 Lewis published, under a pseudonym, A Grief Observed, *the extraordinarily honest and observant notebooks about his early weeks of bereavement. They are often bitter and full of his own psychological wounds, but they tell of a journey in faith. He refers to Joy in the book as 'H'.*

No one ever told me about the laziness of grief. Except at my job – where the machine seems to run on much as usual – I loathe the slightest effort. Not only writing but even reading a letter is too much. Even shaving. What does it matter now whether my cheek is rough or smooth? They say an unhappy man wants distractions – something to take him out of himself. Only as a dog-tired man wants an extra blanket on a cold night; he'd rather lie there shivering than get up and find one. It's easy to see why the lonely become untidy; finally, dirty and disgusting.

Meanwhile, where is God? This is one of the most disquieting symptoms. When you are happy, so happy that you have no sense of needing Him, so happy that you are tempted to feel His claims upon you as an interruption, if you remember yourself and turn to Him with gratitude and praise, you will be – or so it feels – welcomed with open arms. But go to Him when your need is desperate, when all other help is vain, and what do you find? A door slammed in your face, and a sound of bolting and double bolting on the inside. After that, silence. You may as well turn away. The longer you wait, the more emphatic the silence will become. There are no lights in the windows. It might be an empty house. . . .

And grief still feels like fear. Perhaps, more strictly, like suspense. Or like waiting; just hanging about waiting for something to happen. It gives life a permanently provisional feeling. It doesn't seem worth starting anything. I can't settle down. I yawn, I fidget, I smoke too much. Up till this I always had too little time. Now there is nothing but time. Almost pure time, empty successiveness. . . .

I have gradually been coming to feel that the door is no longer shut and bolted. Was it my own frantic need that slammed it in my face? The time when there is nothing at all in your soul except a cry for help may be just the time when God can't give it: you are like the drowning man who can't be helped because he clutches and grabs. Perhaps your own reiterated cries deafen you to the voice you hoped to hear. . . .

When I lay questions before God I get no answer. But a rather special sort of 'No answer'. It is not the locked door. It is more like a silent, certainly not uncompassionate, gaze. As though He shook His head not in refusal but waiving the question. Like, 'Peace, child; you don't understand.'

Can a mortal ask questions which God finds unanswerable? Quite easily, I should think. All nonsense questions are unanswerable. How many hours are there in a mile? Is yellow square or round? Probably half the questions we ask – half our great theological and metaphysical problems – are like that.

And now that I come to think of it, there's no practical problem before me at all. I know the two great commandments, and I'd better get on with them. Indeed, H's death has ended the practical problem. While she was alive I could, in practice, have put her before God; that is, could have done what she wanted instead of what He wanted; if there'd been a conflict. What's left is not a problem about anything I could do. It's all about weights of feelings and motives and that sort of thing. It's a problem I'm setting myself. I don't believe God set it me at all.

The fruition of God. Re-union with the dead. These can't figure in my thinking except as counters. Blank cheques. My idea – if you can call it an idea – of the first is a huge, risky extrapolation from a very few and short experiences here on earth. Probably not such valuable experiences as I think. Perhaps even of less value than others that I take no account of. My idea of the second is also an extrapolation. The reality of either – the cashing of either cheque – would probably blow all one's ideas about both (how much more one's ideas about their relations to each other) into smithereens.

The mystical union on the one hand. The resurrection of the body, on the other. I can't reach the ghost of an image, a formula, or even a feeling, that combines them. But the reality, we are given to understand, does. Reality the iconoclast once more. Heaven will solve our problems, but not, I think, by showing us subtle reconciliations between all our apparently contradictory notions. The notions will all be knocked from under our feet. We shall see that there never was any problem.

And, more than once, that impression which I can't describe except by saying that it's like the sound of a chuckle in the darkness. The sense that some shattering and disarming simplicity is the real answer.

The sea at Brighton
Samuel Johnson

Samuel Johnson (1709–84) was admired as a literary figure of his age, compiling his monumental dictionary, writing poetry, biography, essays and criticism. But in his efforts to practise a Christian life he struggled with a strain of melancholy. He married, at 26, Elizabeth ('Tetty') Porter, 20 years his elder. She died 17 years later, and he always felt the loss. Brighthelmston in the diary entry here is now called Brighton.

1770 March 28, Wednesday   This is the day on which in '52 I was deprived of poor dear Tetty. Having left off the practice of thinking on her with some particular combinations, I have recalled her to my mind of late less frequently, but when I recollect the time in which we lived together, my grief for her departure is not abated, and I have less pleasure in any good that befalls me, because she does not partake it. On many occasions I think what she would have said or done. When I saw the sea at Brighthelmston, I wished for her to have seen it with me. But with respect to her no rational wish is now left but that we may meet at last where the mercy of God shall make us happy, and perhaps make us instrumental to the happiness of each other. It is now eighteen years.

What I had seen
P.J. Kavanagh

P.J. Kavanagh (born 1931) is a poet and writer who lives in Gloucestershire. His memoir The Perfect Stranger *won the Richard Hillary Prize in 1966. In it he writes of his first wife, Sally, who died in 1958. The poem below appears in his* Collected Poems *(1992).*

Beyond Decoration

      Stalled, in the middle of a rented room,
      The couple who own it quarrelling in the yard
      Outside, about which shade of Snowcem
      They should use. (From the bed I'd heard
      Her say she liked me in my dressing-gown
      And heard her husband's grunt of irritation.
      Some ladies like sad men who are alone.)
      But I am stalled, and sad is not the word.
      Go out I cannot, nor can I stay in,
      Becalmed mid-carpet, breathless, on the road
      To nowhere and the road has petered out.
      This was twenty years ago, and bad as that.
      I must have moved at last, for I knelt down,
      Which I had not before, nor thought I should.
      It would not be exact to say I prayed;
      What for? The one I wanted there was dead.
      All I could do was kneel and so I did.
      At once I entered dark so vast and warm
      I wondered it could fit inside the room
      When I looked round. The road I had to walk down
      Was still there. From that moment it was mean
      Beyond my strength to doubt what I had seen:
      A heat at the heart of dark, so plainly shown,
      A bowl, of two cupped hands, in which a pain
      That filled a room could be engulfed and drown
      And yet, for truth is in the bowl, remain . . .

Today I thought it time to write this down,
Beyond decoration, humble, in plain rhyme,
As clear as I could, and as truthful, which I have done.

Loud voice for singing
Hilaire Belloc

Hilaire Belloc (1870–1953) was an opinionated historian and voluminous author. He walked across America to woo Elodie Hogan, whom he married in 1896. She died in 1914. In 'The Winged Horse', a song which he can be heard singing in a loud but reedy voice on a surviving recording, his wounded soul defies sorrow in a very Bellocian way.

The Winged Horse

It's ten years ago today you turned me out o' doors
To cut my feet on flinty lands and stumble down the shores,
And I thought about the all-in-all, oh more than I can tell!
But I caught a horse to ride upon and I rode him very well,
He had flame behind the eyes of him and wings upon his side.
And I ride, and I ride!

I rode him out of Wantage and I rode him up the hill,
And there I saw the Beacon in the morning standing still,
Inkpen and Hackpen and southward and away
High through the middle airs in the strengthening of the day,
And there I saw the channel-glint and England in her pride.
And I ride, and I ride!

And once a-top of Lambourne Down toward the hill of Clere
I saw the Host of Heaven in rank and Michael with his spear,
And Turpin out of Gascony and Charlemagne the Lord,
And Roland of the marches with his hand upon his sword
For the time he should have need of it, and forty more beside.
And I ride, and I ride!

For you that took the all-in-all the things you left were three.
A loud voice for singing and keen eyes to see,
And a spouting well of joy within that never yet was dried!
And I ride.

We'll try to understand
Dorothy L. Sayers

Dorothy L. Sayers (1893–1957) wrote detective novels that remain immensely popular. Her radio drama The Man Born to be King, *broadcast during the Second World War, made a stir. She also translated Dante's* Divine Comedy *with excellect short notes.*

God's Lent Child

'I'll lend you for a little while, a child of mine,' God said.
'For you to love while he lives, and mourn for when he's
        dead.
He may be six or seven years, or forty-two or three,
But will you till I call him back, take care of him for me?
He'll bring his charms to gladden you, and should his stay
        be brief
You'll always have his memories as a solace in your grief
I cannot promise he will stay, for all from earth return
But there are lessons taught below I want this child to learn.
I've looked this whole world over in my search for teachers
        true
And from the folk that crowd Life's lane, I have chosen you.
Now will you give him all your love and not think the labour
        vain,
Nor hate me when I come to take this lent child back again?'

I fancy that I heard them say 'Dear God, Thy will be done.
We will shield him with tenderness, we'll love him while
        we may.

95

And for all the happiness we've known, we'll ever grateful
    stay.
But should the angels call him much sooner than we'd
    planned
We'll brave the bitter grief that comes and try to understand.'

Naught to weep for
John Clare

*John Clare (1793–1864) left among his notes a touching list of the chapbooks
he planned to give his children for Christmas (Frederic:* Peacock at Home
and Butterflyes Ball*). He and his wife had nine children of whom seven
survived infancy. He wrote the poem below in 1844, when detained in Northamptonshire asylum.*

Infants' graves are steps of angels, where
Earth's brightest gems of innocence repose.
God is their parent, and they need no tear,
He takes them to his bosom from earth's woes,
A bud their lifetime and a flower their close.
Their spirits are an Iris of the skies,
Needing no prayers; a sunset's happy close,
Gone are the bright rays of their soft blue eyes;
Flowers weep in dewdrops o'er them, and the gale
    gently sighs.
Their lives were nothing but a sunny shower,
Melting on flowers as tears melt from the eye,
Their deaths were dewdrops on heaven's amaranth bower,
And tolled on flowers as summer gales went by.
They bowed and trembled, and they left no sigh,
And the sun smiled to show their end was well.
Infants have naught to weep for ere they die;
All prayers are needless, beads they need not tell,
White flowers their mourners are, nature their passing-bell.

Finding forgiveness

Too heavy for me to bear
Psalm 38

Psalm 38 (37 according to the Vulgate numbering) appears in the Book of Common Prayer in the version translated by Miles Coverdale (1488–1569) for the Great Bible of 1539. The very strangeness of some of the phraseology ('I have roared for the very disquietness of my heart') increases its power of expressing awareness of sin and trust in God. Most of the psalms are strongly comforting, all the more so through the familiarity that comes through habitual recitation, whether in Hebrew, Latin or English.

1. Put me not to rebuke, O Lord, in thine anger: neither chasten me in thy heavy displeasure.
2. For thine arrows stick fast in me: and thy hand presseth me sore.
3. There is no health in my flesh, because of thy displeasure: neither is there any rest in my bones, by reason of my sin.
4. For my wickednesses are gone over my head: and are like a sore burden, too heavy for me to bear.
5. My wounds stink, and are corrupt: through my foolishness.
6. I am brought into so great trouble and misery: that I go mourning all the day long.
7. For my loins are filled with a sore disease: and there is no whole part in my body.
8. I am feeble, and sore smitten: I have roared for the very disquietness of my heart.
9. Lord, thou knowest all my desire: and my groaning is not hid from thee.
10. My heart panteth, my strength hath failed me: and the sight of mine eyes is gone from me.

11. My lovers and my neighbours did stand looking upon my trouble: and my kinsmen stood afar off.

12. They also that sought after my life laid snares for me: and they that went about to do me evil talked of wickedness, and imagined deceit all the day long.

13. As for me I was like a deaf men, and heard not: and as one that is dumb, who doth not open his mouth.

14. I became even as a man that heareth not: and in whose mouth are no reproofs.

15. For in thee, O Lord, have I put my trust: thou shalt answer for me, O Lord my God.

16. I have required that they, even mine enemies should not triumph over me: for when my foot slipped, they rejoiced greatly against me.

17. And I, truly, am set in the plague: and my heaviness is ever in my sight.

18. For I will confess my wickedness: and be sorry for my sin.

19. But mine enemies live, and are mighty: and they that hate me wrongfully are many in number.

20. They also that reward evil for good are against me: because I follow the thing that good is.

21. Forsake me not, O Lord my God: be not thou far from me.

22. Haste thee to help me: O Lord God of my salvation.

Hope is the window
John Fisher

John Fisher (1469–1535) was a leading academic of his time, being elected Master of Michaelhouse, Cambridge, and the first Lady Margaret Professor of Divinity at Cambridge University. In 1504 he became Chancellor of Cambridge University and Bishop of Rochester. In that year he composed his Exposition of the Seven Penitential Psalms. *Traditionally Psalms 6, 31, 37, 50, 101, 129 and 142 (in the Vulgate numbering) were employed to express sorrow for sin. Fisher was beheaded by Henry VIII in 1535.*

Psalm 37 (38 in the King James Version)

Verse 15: *Quoniam in te, Domine, speravi. Tu exaudies, Domine Deus meus.*

'Lorde, thou shalte hear me bycause I have trusted in thee.'

Hytherto our prophet [David] hath described the miserable and unhappy condycions of the synner, expressynge his manyfolde wretchednesses. Now in this seconde place he remembreth many thynges whereby the goodness of God may be moved to forgyveness, amongst which good hope is the fyrst, without the which every thynge that we do is of no valure, for let us never so much wail and sorrow our synnes, confess them to never so many preestes and study to purge them by as much satysfaccyon as we can, all these profyte no thynge without hope.

For was not Judas very penytent for his synnes? Yes truly. For as Mathewe sayth: Iudas penitencia ductus rettulit triginta argenteos principibus sacerdotum; 'Iudas beynge penytent brought agayne the 30 pens to the prynces of preestes, or to the chefe of the Jewes lawe.' Dyde he not also shewe openly his trespasse when he made exclamacyon and sayd: Peccavi tradens sanguinem iustum; 'I have synned grevously betrayenge this ryghtwyse blode'? And laste he made satisfaccyon more large than almyghty God wolde have asked. Abiens laqueo se suspendit; 'He wente forth and hanged hymselfe in an halter.'

I beseche you what more bytter and shamefull kynde of satysfaccyon might have fortuned him? Veryly none. And yet bycause he wanted hope and despayred of forgyveness, all these dyde no thynge profyte hym. For without doubte desperacyon is so thycke an obstacle, unless it be taken away, the lyght of Goddes grace may not come in to our soules. Let us therefore take awaye the obstacle of despayre and open our soules by stedfast hope to receyve the grace of God, and it must needes enter.

Saynt Paule sayth: Deus negare seipsum non potest; 'Almyghty God may not deny his owne selfe', he can not but have mercy on wretched synners that truste in hym. He may no more withdrawe from them the bemes of his grace, yf theyr soules be made open by stedfast hope to receyve it, than the sun may withstande his bemes out of wyndowes whan they be open.

Therefore the prophete sayth: Quoniam in te domine speravi. Tu exaudies me Domine Deus meus; 'Blessed Lorde, bycause I have trusted in thee, thou shalte here me, my Lord and my God.' Of a truth, great and stedfast hope must needs alwaye be heard, notwithstandynge these fewe condycyons followynge must be joyned to it: that is to saye, yf the thynge asked of almyghty God be longynge and not contrary to the soules health of the asker; also if he be wyllynge and ready to suffre correction for his synnes; yf he sorrowe and waile his errour and be gladde to accuse hymselfe. Last yf he wyll beware and from that tyme forthwarde abstayne from all suche evyll occasyon.

All these the prophete remembred by the same order, and made his petycyon for to be heard of almyghty God, and showed the cause why be sholde be heard, sayenge: Quoniam in te domine speravi; 'Lorde, thou shalte hear me bycause I have trusted in thee.'

Happy fault
The Exsultet

The Exsultet is an ancient song of praise sung before the lit paschal candle during the darkness of the vigil on the eve of Easter. There are references to this song from the fourth century. The fire of the flame represents the glory of the risen Christ. The song unites the Passover of the Old Testament with the liberation from sin and death brought by Christ's sacrifice. The wonder of the incarnation of God as a man makes the narrator exclaim daringly O felix culpa, 'Happy sin of Adam that brought us such a Redeemer'.

This is our Passover feast,
When Christ, the true Lamb, is slain,
whose blood consecrates the homes of all believers.

This is the night,
when first you saved our fathers:
you freed the people of Israel from their slavery,
and led them dry-shod through the sea.

This is the night,
when the pillar of fire destroyed the darkness of sin.

This is night,
when Christians everywhere,
washed clean of sin and freed from all defilement,
are restored to grace and grow together in holiness.

This is the night,
when Jesus broke the chains of death
and rose triumphant from the grave.

What good would life have been to us,
had Christ not come as our Redeemer?

Father, how wonderful your care for us!
How boundless your merciful love!
To ransom a slave you gave away your Son.

O happy fault, O necessary sin of Adam,
which gained for us so great a Redeemer!

Most blessed of all nights,
chosen by God to see Christ rising from the dead!

Of this night scripture says:
'The night will be as clear as day:
it will become my light, my joy.'

The power of this holy night dispels all evil,
washes guilt away,

restores lost innocence,
brings mourners joy;
it casts out hatred,
brings us peace,
and humbles earthly pride.

Night truly blessed,
when heaven is wedded to earth
and we are reconciled to God!

Stings and honey
Edward Taylor

*Edward Taylor (1642–1729), a convinced Calvinist Puritan, left England in
1668 and became a minister in Massachusetts. He would prepare for the
monthly service of Communion by composing for his own use a meditation in
verse. Most of his poetry remained unpublished until the 20th century but has
now become a favourite of university courses. His style is often awkward but
his sincerity is compelling. 'The soul's groan' and 'Christ's reply' come from
his long sequence God's Determinations, probably finished in about 1680.*

The soul's groan to Christ for succour

Good Lord, behold this Dreadfull Enemy
Who makes me tremble with his fierce assaults:
I dare not trust, yet feare to give the ly,
For in my soul, my soul finds many faults,
And though I justify myselfe to's face:
I do Condemn myselfe before thy Grace.

He strives to mount my sins, and them advance
Above thy Merits, Pardons, or Good Will;
Thy Grace to lessen, and thy Wrath t' inhance
As if thou couldst not pay the sinner's bill,

He Chiefly injures thy rich Grace, I finde,
Though I confess my heart to sin inclin'de.

Those Graces which thy Grace enwrought in mee,
He makes as nothing but a pack of Sins;
He maketh Grace no grace, but Crueltie;
Is Grace's Honey Comb, a Comb of Stings?
This makes me ready leave thy Grace and run,
Which if I do, I finde I am undone.

I know he is thy Cur, therefore I bee
Perplexed lest I from thy Pasture stray,
He bayghs and barks so veh'mently at mee.
Come, rate this Cur, Lord, breake his teeth I pray.
Remember me I humbly pray thee first,
Then halter up this Cur that is so Curst.

Christ's reply

Peace, Peace, my Hony, do not Cry,
My Little Darling, wipe thine eye,
Oh Cheer, Cheer up, come see.
Is anything too deare, my Dove,
Is anything too good, my Love,
To get or give for thee?

If in the severall thou art,
This Yelper fierce will at thee bark:
That thou art mine this shows.
As Spot barks back the sheep again,
Before they to the Pound are ta'ne,
So he, and hence 'way goes.

But if this Cur that bayghs so sore,
Is broken tootht, and muzzled sure,
Fear not, my Pritty Heart.

His barking is to make thee Cling
Close underneath thy Saviours wing.
Why did my sweeten start?

And if he run an inch too fur,
I'le Check his Chain, and rate the Cur.
My Chick, keep close to mee.
The Poles shall sooner kiss and greet
And Paralells shall sooner meet,
Than thou shall harmed bee.

He seeks to aggrivate thy sin,
And screw them to the highest pin,
To make thy faith to quaile.
Yet mountain sins like mites should show,
And then these mites for naught should goe,
Could he but once prevaile.

I smote thy sins upon the Head.
They Dead'ned are, though not quite dead.
And shall not rise again.
I'l put away the Guilt thereof,
And purge its Filthiness cleare off:
My Blood doth out the stain.

And though thy judgment was remiss,
Thy Headstrong Will too Wilfull is:
I will Renew the same.
And though thou do too frequently
Offend as heretofore, hereby
I'le not severely blaim.

And though thy senses do inveagle
Thy Noble Soul to tend the Beagle,
That t' hunt her games forthgo.

I'le Lure her back to me, and Change
Those fond Affections that do range
As yelping beagles doe.

Although thy sins increase their race,
And though when thou hast sought for Grace,
Thou fallst more than before:
If thou by true Repentance Rise,
And Faith makes me thy Sacrifice,
I'l pardon all, though more.

Though Satan strive to block thy way
By all his Stratagems he may,
Come, come, though through the fire.
For Hell, that Gulph of fire for sins,
Is not so hot as t' burn thy Shins,
Then Credit not the Lyar.

Those Cursed Vermin Sins that Crawl
All ore thy Soul, both Greate and Small,
Are onely Satan's own:
Which he in his Malignity
Unto thy Soul's true Sanctity
In at the doore hath thrown.

And though they be Rebellion high,
Ath'ism or Apostacy:
Though blasphemy it bee:
Unto what quality, or Sise,
Excepting one, so e're it rise,
Repent, I'le pardon thee.

Although thy Soule was once a Stall
Rich hung with Satan's nicknacks all;
If thou Repent thy Sin,

A Tabernacle in 't I'le place,
Fill'd with God's Spirit, and his Grace.
Oh Comfortable thing!

I dare the World therefore to show
A God like me, to anger slow:
Whose wrath is full of Grace.
Doth hate all Sins both Greate and Small:
Yet when Repented, pardons all.
Frowns with a Smiling Face.

As for thy outward Postures each,
Thy Gestures, Actions, and thy Speech,
I Eye, and Eying spare,
If thou repent. My Grace is more
Ten thousand times still tribled ore
Than thou canst want, or ware.

As for the Wicked Charge he makes,
That he of Every Dish first takes
Of all thy holy things:
It's false; deny the same, and say,
That which he had he stool away
Out of thy Offerings.

Though to thy Griefe, poor Heart, thou finde
In Pray're too oft a wandring minde,
In Sermons, Spirits dull:
Though faith in firy furnace flags,
And Zeale in Chilly Seasons lags:
Temptations powerfull:

These faults are his, and none of thine
So fur as thou dost them decline:
Come then, receive my Grace.

And when he buffits thee therefore,
If thou my aid and Grace implore,
I'le shew a pleasant face.

But still look for Temptations Deep,
Whilst that thy Noble Sparke doth keep
Within a Mudwald Cote.
These White Frosts and the Showers that fall
Are but to whiten thee withall,
Not rot the Web they smote,

If in the fire where Cold is tri'de,
Thy Soule is put, and purifi'de,
Wilt thou lament thy loss?
If silver-like this fire refine
Thy Soul and make it brighter Shine:
Wilt thou bewaile the Dross?

Oh! fight my Field: no Colours fear:
I'l be thy Front, I'l be thy reare.
Fail not: my Battells fight.
Defy the Tempter, and his Mock.
Anchor thy heart on mee, thy Rock.
I do in thee Delight.

Be comforted
Rorate coeli

'Rorate coeli desuper et nubes pluant justum' are the first words of verse 8 in the 45th chapter of the prophet Isaiah. The translation 'Drop dew, ye heavens, from above and let the clouds rain the Just One,' sounds strange, but justum is taken as referring to the coming Messiah, Christ. The words were used at antiphons

in Advent and as the refrain to a traditional set of prayers contemplating sin, desolation, the affliction of God's people, and God's consolation of them by sending a saviour.

Ne irascaris Domine, ne ultra memineris iniquitatis
Ecce civitas Sancti facta est deserta
Sion deserta facta est: Jerusalem desolata est
Domus sanctificationis tuae et gloriae tuae
Ubi laudaverunt te patres nostri.

Rorate coeli desuper et nubes pluant justum

Be not very angry, O Lord, and remember no longer our
    iniquity:
Behold, thy holy city is become deserted;
Sion is become a desert; Jerusalem is desolate;
The house of thy sanctification and thy glory,
Where our fathers praised thee.

Drop dew, ye heavens, from above and let the clouds rain
    the Just One.

Peccavimus, et facti sumus tamquam immundus nos
Et cecidimus, quasi folium universi
Et iniquitates nostrae quasi ventus abstulerunt nos
Abscondisti faciem tuam a nobis
Et allisisti nos in manu iniquitatis nostrae.

Rorate coeli desuper et nubes pluant justum

We have sinned and are become as unclean:
We have all fallen as a leaf
And our iniquities like the wind have carried us away.
Thou hast hidden Thy face from us,
And hast crushed us in the hand of our iniquity.

108

Drop dew, ye heavens, from above and let the clouds rain
    the Just One.

Vide Domine afflictionem populi tui
Et mitte quem missurus es;
Emitte Agnum dominatorem terrae
De Petra deserti ad montem filiae Sion
Ut auferat ipse jugum captivitatis nostrae.

Rorate coeli desuper et nubes pluant justum

Behold, O Lord, the affliction of Thy people
And send forth Him who is to come:
Send forth the Lamb, the ruler of the earth
From Petra of the desert to the mount of the daughter
    of Sion:
That He may take away the yoke of our captivity.

Drop dew, ye heavens, from above and let the clouds rain
    the Just One.

Consolamini, consolamini, popule meus
Cito veniet salus tua: Quare moerore consumeris
Quia innovavit te dolor? Salvabo te, noli timere
Ego enim sum Dominus Deus tuus,
Sanctus Israel, redemptor.

Rorate coeli desuper et nubes pluant justum

Be comforted, be comforted, my people:
Thy salvation cometh quickly: why with grief art thou
    consumed
Because sorrow hath stricken thee? I will save thee, fear not:
For I am the Lord thy God,
The Holy One of Israel, thy Redeemer.

Drop dew, ye heavens, from above and let the clouds rain
the Just One.

I smell the dew
George Herbert

*George Herbert (1593–1633) considers the reblossoming of a shrivelled heart,
and of his powers of writing poetry. He does so by exercising the image of a
flower for all it's worth.*

The Flower

How fresh, O Lord, how sweet and clean
Are thy returns! ev'n as the flowers in spring;
To which, besides their own demean,
The late-past frosts tributes of pleasure bring.
Grief melts away
Like snow in May,
As if there were no such cold thing.

Who would have thought my shrivelled heart
Could have recovered greenness? It was gone
Quite under ground; as flowers depart
To see their mother-root, when they have blown;
Where they together
All the hard weather,
Dead to the world, keep house unknown.

These are thy wonders, Lord of power,
Killing and quick'ning, bringing down to hell
And up to heaven in an hour;
Making a chiming of a passing-bell.
We say amiss,
This or that is:
Thy word is all, if we could spell.

O that I once past changing were,
Fast in thy Paradise, where no flower can wither!
Many a spring I shoot up fair,
Off'ring at heaven, growing and groaning thither.
Nor doth my flower
Want a spring-shower,
My sins and I joining together.

But while I grow in a straight line,
Still upwards bent, as if heaven were mine own,
Thy anger comes, and I decline;
What frost to that? what pole is not the zone,
Where all things burn,
When thou dost turn,
And the least frown of thine is shown?

And now in age I bud again,
After so many deaths I live and write;
I once more smell the dew and rain,
And relish versing: O my only light,
It cannot be
That I am he
On whom thy tempests fell all night.

These are thy wonders, Lord of love,
To make us see we are but flowers that glide:
Which when we once can find and prove,
Thou hast a garden for us, where to bide.
Who would be more,
Swelling through store,
Forfeit their Paradise by their pride.

The world a prison

The door shut
Thomas More

Thomas More (1477–1535) was a Renaissance humanist, the first layman to become Lord Chancellor, a wit, a scholar and a saint. He ended his life a martyr because there was a step in his career that in conscience he would not tread; he stopped, resigned, settled his affairs and waited for imprisonment, a show-trial and death.

In the Tower he wrote A Dialogue of Comfort Against Tribulation. *The dialogue is between Anthony and his nephew Vincent. The question under discussion is how to keep faith in God if the Turks invade and put pressure on you, even to imprisonment and death, to deny Christianity. For More it was no Turk but the King himself who wanted to him to break faith in the matter of the divorce from Queen Catherine.*

More's book reflects his lawyerly background: questions are thrown about and objections lodged on either side, as if it were a game. But for him it was deadly earnest. At one point the nephew tells his uncle he is not convinced in his heart by his elder's arguments. More feared physical pain and violent death.

So this is one of the most personal of all More's works. The woman who liked to shut up her own room snugly and yet felt stifled in a prison cell if the door was closed is More's own wife.

Earlier in the dialogue More goes as far as to argue that God is our jailer. At first this seems an outrageous claim, as if God hated us. But More means that if men complain of cramped limbs in a real prison, are they not as likely to suffer crippled limbs from disease or mischance outside, when supposedly free? If God's Providence decrees the prison-irons or the crippling, then we must trust that it is no more than we can bear and that it is for the good. Jesus Christ himself suffered imprisonment and ill-treatment. In any case, if we reject faith now, how shall that help us suffer less?

More's analysis is applicable to present-day 'imprisonment' through old age, immobility, hospitalization and loss of independence — and to plain imprisonment if it comes to it.

ANTHONY: And surely, as we think ourselves out of prison now, so if there were some folk born and brought up in a prison, who never came on the wall or looked out at the door or heard of another world outside, but saw some, for ill turns done among themselves, locked up in straiter room; and if they heard them alone called prisoners who were so served and themselves ever called free folk at large, the like opinion would they have there of themselves then as we have here of ourselves now. And when we take ourselves for other than prisoners now, verily are we now as deceived as those prisoners would be then.

VINCENT: But yet, since, for all this, there appeareth no more but that as they are prisoners so are we too, and that as some of them are sore handled so are some of us too; we know well, for all this, that when we come to those prisons we shall not fail to be in a straiter prison than we are now, and to have a door shut upon us where we have none shut on us now. This shall we be sure of at least if there come no worse — and then may there come worse, you know well, since it cometh there so commonly. And therefore is it yet little marvel that men's hearts grudge much against it.

ANTHONY: Surely, cousin, in this you say very well. Howbeit, your words would have touched me somewhat the nearer if I had said that imprisonment were no displeasure at all. But the thing that I say, cousin, for our comfort in the matter, is that our fancy frameth us a false opinion by which we deceive ourselves and take it for sorer than it is. And that we do because we take ourselves for more free before than we are, and imprisonment for a stranger thing to us than it is indeed. And thus far, as I say, I have proved truth in very deed.

113

But now the incommodities that you repeat again – those, I say, that are proper to the imprisonment of its own nature; that is, to have less room to walk in and to have the door shut upon us – these are, methinketh, so very slender and slight that in so great a cause as to suffer for God's sake we might be sore ashamed so much as once to think upon them.

Many a good man there is, you know, who, without any force at all, or any necessity wherefore he should do so, suffereth these two things willingly of his own choice, with much other hardness more. Holy monks, I mean, of the Charterhouse order, such as never pass their cells save only to the Church, which is set fast by their cells, and thence to their cells again. And St Brigit's order, and St Clare's much alike, and in a manner all enclosed religious houses. And yet anchorites and anchoresses most especially, all whose whole room is less than a good large chamber. And yet are they there as well content many long years together as are other men – and better, too – who walk about the world. And therefore you may see that the lothness of less room and the door shut upon us, since so many folk are so well content with them and will for God's love choose to live so, is but a horror enhanced of our own fancy.

And indeed I knew a woman once who came into a prison, to visit of her charity a poor prisoner there. She found him in a chamber that was fair enough, to say the truth – at least, it was strong enough! But with mats of straw the prisoner had made it so warm, both under foot and round about the walls, that in these things, for the keeping of his health, she was on his behalf glad and very well comforted. But among many other displeasures that for his sake she was sorry for, one she lamented much in her mind. And that was that he should have the chamber door made fast upon him by night, by the jailor who was to shut him in. 'For, by my troth,' quoth she, 'if the door should be shut upon me, I think it would stop up my breath!' At that word of hers the prisoner laughed in his mind – but he dared not laugh aloud or say anything to her, for indeed he stood somewhat in awe of her, and he had his food there in great part of her charity for alms. But he could not but laugh inwardly, for he knew well enough that she used to shut her own chamber door full surely on the inside every night, both door and windows too, and used not to open them all the long night. And what difference, then, as to the stopping of the breath, whether they were shut up within or without?

As for those other accidents of hard handling, I am not so mad as to say that they are no grief, but I say that our fear may imagine them much greater grief than they are. And I say that such as they be, many a man endureth them – yea, and many a woman too – who afterward fareth full well.

And then would I know what determination we take – whether for our Saviour's sake to suffer some pain in our bodies, since he suffered in his blessed body so great pain for us, or else to give him warning and be at a point utterly to forsake him rather than to suffer any pain at all? He who cometh in his mind unto this latter point – from which kind of unkindness God keep every man! – he needeth no comfort, for he will flee the need. And counsel, I fear, availeth him little, if grace be so far gone from him. But, on the other hand, if, rather than to forsake our Saviour, we determine ourselves to suffer any pain at all, I cannot then see that the fear of hard handling should anything stick with us and make us to shrink so that we would rather forsake his faith than suffer for his sake so much as imprisonment. For the handling is neither such in prison but what many men, and many women too, live with it many years and sustain it, and afterward yet fare full well.

And yet it may well fortune that, beside the bare imprisonment, there shall happen to us no hard handling at all. Or else it may happen to us for only a short while – and yet, beside all this, peradventure not at all. And which of all these ways shall be taken with us, lieth all in his will for whom we are content to take it, and who for that intent of ours favoureth us and will suffer no man to put more pain unto us than he well knoweth we shall be able to bear. For he himself will give us the strength for it, as you have heard his promise already by the mouth of St Paul: 'God is faithful, who suffereth you not to be tempted above what you may bear, but giveth also with the temptation a way out.'

But now, if we have not lost our faith already before we come to forsake it for fear, we know very well by our faith that, by the forsaking of our faith, we fall into that state to be cast into the prison of hell. And that can we not tell how soon; but, as it may be that God will suffer us to live a while here upon earth, so may it be that he will throw us into that dungeon beneath before the time that the Turk shall once ask us the question. And therefore, if we fear imprisonment so sore, we are much more than mad if we fear not most the imprisonment that is far more sore. For out of that prison shall no man never get, and in this other shall no man abide but a while.

In prison was Joseph while his brethren were at large; and yet afterward were his brethren fain to seek upon him for bread. In prison was Daniel, and the wild lions about him; and yet even there God kept him harmless and brought him safe out again. If we think that he will not do the like for us, let us not doubt but that he will do for us either the like or better, for better may he do for us if he suffer us there to die. St John the Baptist was, you know, in prison, while Herod and Herodias sat full merry at the feast, and the daughter of Herodias delighted them with her dancing, till with her dancing she danced off St John's head. And now sitteth he with great feast in heaven at God's board, while Herod and Herodias full heavily sit in hell burning both twain, and to make them sport withal the devil with the damsel dance in the fire before them.

Finally, cousin, to finish this piece, our Saviour was himself taken prisoner for our sake. And prisoner was he carried, and prisoner was he kept, and prisoner was he brought forth before Annas, and prisoner from Annas carried unto Caiphas. Then prisoner was he carried from Caiphas unto Pilate, and prisoner was he sent from Pilate to King Herod, and prisoner from Herod unto Pilate again. And so was he kept as prisoner to the end of his passion. The time of his imprisonment, I grant you, was not long. But as for hard handling, which our hearts most abhor, he had as much in that short while as many men among them all in a much longer time. And surely, then, if we consider of what estate he was and also that he was prisoner in that wise for our sake, we shall, I think, unless we be worse than wretched beasts, never so shamefully play the ungrateful coward as sinfully to forsake him for fear of imprisonment.

Nor shall we be so foolish either as, by forsaking him, to give him the occasion to forsake us in turn. For so should we, with the avoiding of an easier prison, fall into a worse. And instead of the prison that cannot keep us long, we should fall into that prison out of which we can never come, though the short imprisonment should have won us everlasting liberty.

To blossom again
John Clare

John Clare (1793–1864) writes from detention in a lunatic asylum. He sees nature as God's pledge of enduring love and its future blossoming.

Summer morning is risen
And to even it wends,
And still I'm in prison
Without any friends.

I had joy's assurance
Though in bondage I lie –
I am still left in durance,
Unwilling to sigh.

Still the forest is round me
Where the trees bloom in green,
As if chains ne'er had bound me
Or cares had ne'er been.

Nature's love is eternal
In forest and plain,

117

Her course is diurnal
To blossom again.

For home and friends vanished,
I have kindness not wrath,
For in days care has banished
My heart possessed both.

My hopes are all hopeless,
My skies have no sun,
Winter fell in youth's May Day,
And still freezes on;

But love like the seed is
In the heart of a flower,
It will blossom in truth
In a prosperous hour.

True love is eternal,
For God is the giver,
And love like the soul will
Endure – and for ever.

Not in a dungeon
Christopher Smart

Christopher Smart (1722–71) confronted some of the hardships, frustrations and fears of being declared mad in his remarkable long poem Jubilate Agno, 'Rejoice in the Lamb'. Its main purpose is adoration. Smart was already a prize-winning poet, who had produced his own metrical version of the Psalms. When he was earning his living as a hack writer he gained the reputation for crankiness. His fellow hack, Samuel Johnson, who himself knew something of melancholy madness, defended him: 'Although, rationally speaking, it is greater madness not to pray at all than to pray as Smart did, I am afraid there are so many people who do not pray that their understanding is not called in question.'

From 1756 to 1763 Smart was under some sort of constraint, for a time at St Luke's, at other times probably in private asylums. He had been too ill to work, he was drinking too much and showing some sort of religious mania, and his family could not cope with him.

Jubilate Agno was presumably composed between the earliest date mentioned in its text, August 13 1759, and the latest, January 30 1763. The best known passage in it is the one beginning 'For I shall consider my cat, Jeoffry', a charming, prayerful consideration of the creature.

But Jubilate Agno was written antiphonally, as if for alternate recital by two choirs on each side of a chapel. Smart wrote the hundreds of lines beginning 'Let' on one bundle of paper, and corresponding lines beginning 'For' on another bundle. Unfortunately more than half the manuscript was lost, and this made it more difficult for later generations to realize that the Let lines matched up with the For lines. The effect of reading the poem disjointedly was to make Smart seem madder than he was. It was not till 1954 that a text edited by W.H. Bond was published tying together the remaining pairs of Let and For lines.

The section below begins with the Apostles named in the New Testament, fishermen, several of them, and so suitably linked each with a fish. Smart was a man of great classical learning, and knowledgeable in natural history. At the end of the extract I have put a few explanatory notes, referring to the numbered pairs of lines.

1. LET PETER rejoice with the MOON FISH who keeps up the life in the waters by night.
For I pray the Lord JESUS that cured the LUNATICK to be merciful to all my brethren and sisters in these houses.

2. Let Andrew rejoice with the Whale, who is array'd in beauteous blue & is a combination of bulk & activity.
For they work me with their harping-irons, which is a barbarous instrument, because I am more unguarded than others.

3. Let James rejoice with the Skuttle-Fish, who foils his foe by the effusion of his ink.

For the blessing of God hath been on my epistles, which I have written for the benefit of others.

4. Let John rejoice with Nautilus who spreads his sail & plies his oar, and the Lord is his pilot.
For I bless God that the CHURCH of ENGLAND is one of the SEVEN ev'n the candlestick of the Lord.

5. Let Philip rejoice with Boca, which is a fish that can speak.
For the ENGLISH TONGUE shall be the language of the WEST.

6. Let Bartholomew rejoice with the Eel, who is pure in proportion to where he is found & how he is used.
For I pray Almighty CHRIST to bless the MAGDALEN HOUSE & to forward a National purification.

7. Let Thomas rejoice with the Sword-Fish, whose aim is perpetual & strength insuperable.
For I have the blessing of God in the three POINTS of manhood, of the pen, of the sword, & of chivalry.

8. Let Matthew rejoice with Uranoscopus, whose eyes are lifted up to God.
For I am inquisitive in the Lord, and defend the philosophy of the scripture against vain deceit.

9. Let James the less, rejoice with the Haddock, who brought the piece of money for the Lord and Peter.
For the nets come down from the eyes of the Lord to fish up men to their salvation.

10. Let Jude bless with the Bream, who is of melancholy from his depth and serenity.
For I have a greater compass both of mirth and melancholy than another.

11. Let Simon rejoice with the Sprat, who is pure and innumerable.
For I bless the Lord JESUS in the innumerables, and for ever & ever.

12. Let Matthias rejoice with the Flying-Fish, who has a part with the birds, and is sublimity in his conceit.

For I am redoubted, and redoubtable in the Lord, as is THOMAS BECKET my father.

13. Let Stephen rejoice with Remora − The Lord remove all obstacles to his glory.

For I have had the grace to GO BACK, which is my blessing unto prosperity.

14. Let Paul rejoice with the Seale, who is pleasant & faithful, like God's good ENGLISHMAN.

For I paid for my out in St PAUL's, when I was six years old, & took possession against the evil day.

15. Let Agrippa, which is Agricola, rejoice with Elops, who is a choice fish.

For I am descended from the steward of the island blessed be the name of the Lord Jesus king of England.

16. Let Joseph rejoice with the Turbut, whose capture makes the poor fisher-man sing.

For the poor gentleman is the first object of the Lord's charity & he is the most pitied who hath lost the most.

17. Let Mary rejoice with the Maid − blessed be the name of the immaculate CONCEPTION.

For I am in twelve HARDSHIPS, but he that was born of a virgin shall deliver me out of all.

18. Let John, the Baptist, rejoice with the Salmon − blessed be the name of the Lord Jesus for infant Baptism.

For I am safe, as to my head, from the female dancer and her admirers.

19. Let Mark rejoice with the Mullet, who is John Dore, God be gracious to him & his family.

For I pray for CHICHESTER to give the glory to God, and to keep the adversary at bay.

20. Let Barnabas rejoice with the Herring – God be gracious to the Lord's fishery.

For I am making to the shore day by day, the Lord Jesus take me.

21. Let Cleopas rejoice with the Mackerel, who cometh in a shoal after a leader.

For I bless the Lord JESUS upon RAMSGATE PIER – the Lord forward the building of harbours.

22. Let Abiud of the Lord's line rejoice with Murex, who is good and of a precious tincture.

For I bless the Lord JESUS for his very seed, which is in my body.

23. Let Eliakim rejoice with the Shad, who is contemned in his abundance.

For I pray for R and his family, I pray for Mr Becher, and I bean for the Lord JESUS.

24. Let Azor rejoice with the Flounder, who is both of the sea and of the river.

For I pray to God for Nore, for the Trinity house, for all light-houses, beacons and buoys.

25. Let Sadoc rejoice with the Bleak, who playeth upon the surface in the Sun.

For I bless God that I am not in a dungeon, but am allowed the light of the Sun.

26. Let Achim rejoice with the Miller's Thumb, who is a delicious morsel for the water fowl.

For I pray God for the PYGMIES against their feather'd adversaries, as a deed of charity.

27. Let Eliud rejoice with Cinaedus, who is a fish yellow all over.

For I pray God for all those, who have defiled themselves in matters inconvenient.

28. Let Eleazar rejoice with the Grampus, who is a pompous spouter.

For I pray God be gracious to CORNELIUS MATTHEWS name & connection.

29. Let Matthan rejoice with the Shark, who is supported by multitudes of small value.
For I am under the same accusation with my Saviour – for they said, he is beside himself.

Notes

2. Smart's mention of 'harping-irons', harpoons, might also refer to physical restraints or medical instruments.
5. Boca was mentioned in medieval bestiaries, and originates, in the form 'box', in Pliny.
13. Remora is a sucking fish, said in myth to be able to stop a ship in full sail and make it go back.
17. The Maid is a kind of skate. Smart seems by mistake to have called the Virgin Birth the Immaculate Conception (which refers to Mary being sinless from the time of her conception). But he was learned in divinity.
18. Salome asked for the head of John the Baptist, and her name might have suggested the salmon.
19. John Dore was held at St Luke's hospital and at Bedlam during Smart's period of confinement. The John Dory is nowadays the name for a different fish from the mullet.
22. Abiud and the names in the following six couplets are taken from the genealogy of St Joseph in St Matthew's gospel.
23. Bean has been interpreted as bene, 'prayer'. But 'bear' could make sense.
26. The Pygmies of myth were at war with the cranes.
29. The accusation comes in Mark 3:21.

Looking forward

How to be really happy
Augustine

Augustine of Hippo (354–430), before he became a Christian, explored the thoughts of the philosophers of his day, whose chief question was: How to be happy. In the extract here, he shows, by a careful build-up of argument, that no one can really be happy unless he is immortal. Without immortality, for which everyone hungers, we can at most put a brave face on things. The argument is not as hard to follow as it first might seem; the style of writing requires only a steady progression from one sentence to the next.

The faith by which we believe in God is particularly necessary in this mortal life, which is so full of delusion and distress and uncertainty. God is the only source to be found of any good things, but especially of those which make a man good and those which will make him happy; only from him do they come into a man and attach themselves to a man. And only when a man who is faithful and good in these unhappy conditions passes from this life to the happy life, will there really and truly be what now cannot possibly be, namely that a man lives as he would.

He will not want to live a bad life in that bliss, nor will he want anything that he lacks, nor will he lack anything that he wants. Whatever he loves will be there, and he will not desire anything that is not there. Everything that is there will be good, and the most high God will be the most high good, and will be available for the enjoyment of his lovers, and thus total happiness will be forever assured.

But now meanwhile the philosophers have all constructed their own happy lives as each has thought best, as though they could manage by their own virtue what they could not manage in their common condition of mortal men, namely to live as they would. They felt indeed that there was no other way for anyone to be happy but by having what he wanted and not enduring anything he did not want. Now, who is there who would not want any kind of life that he enjoyed and thus called happy to be so in his own power that he could have it last forever? And yet who is there in such a position? Does anyone want to suffer troubles he would endure bravely, even though he can endure them if he suffers them? Does anyone want to live in torment, even though he is able to preserve his virtue in it by his patience, and so live laudably?

Those who have endured such evils in their desire to have or their fear to lose what they loved, whether their motive was mean or praiseworthy, have thought that the evils would pass away. Many people have bravely fought their way to abiding good things through transitory evils. Such people are ipso facto happy in hope even in the midst of the transitory evils through which they come to the good things that shall not pass away.

But a man who is happy in hope is not yet happy. He is waiting in patience for the happiness which he does not yet possess. As for the man who is tortured without any such hope, without any such reward, however much endurance he shows, he is not truly happy but bravely unhappy. You cannot say he is not unhappy just because he would be unhappier still if he underwent his unhappiness without patience. Furthermore, he is not even to be regarded as happy if he does not suffer these things he would rather not suffer in his body, because still he is not living as he wants to. To leave aside other things that without harming the body belong to the trials of the mind which we would rather live without (and they are countless in number), he would of course like if possible to have his body so safe and sound without suffering any trouble from it that he had this possibility really under his control, or had it realized in his body's immunity from all decay. Because he has not got this and is held in suspense, clearly he does not live as he would like.

In his courage he may well be prepared to take whatever adversity comes upon him and to bear it with equanimity; but he would

125

prefer it not to come upon him, and if he can he sees to it that it does not. So he is prepared for both eventualities, but in such a way that he hopes for one and avoids the other, and if he runs into the one he would avoid, he willingly bears it because what he wanted would not come about. He endures it therefore in order not to be pushed under completely, but he would rather not be pushed at all.

How then can he be said to live as he would like? Because he is willingly brave in bearing unflinchingly what he would rather had not been inflicted on him? But the reason he wills what he can do is that he cannot do what he wills. That is the sum total, whether it makes you laugh or cry, of the happiness of proud mortals who boast that they live as they want because they bear patiently with what they do not want to happen to them. This, they say, is what Terence put so well: 'Since what you will can never be, will what you can do.'

Who would deny that this is very sensibly said? But it is advice given to an unhappy man how not to be unhappier still. To a happy man, however, such as all men want to be, it is neither right nor true to say what you will can never be. If he is indeed happy, whatever he wants can indeed be, since he does not want what cannot be. But such a state of things is not for this mortal life; it will only be when there is immortality. If this could in no way be given to man, he would look for happiness in vain, because without immortality it cannot be.

All people, then, want to be happy; if they want something true, this necessarily means they want to be immortal. They cannot otherwise be happy. In any case, if you ask them about immortality as about happiness, they all answer that they want it. But as long as they despair of immortality, without which true happiness is impossible, they will look for, or rather make up, any kind of thing that may be called, rather than really be, happiness in this life.

That man lives happily, as we have said above and established firmly enough, who lives as he wants and does not want anything wrongly. But no one is wrong to want immortality if human nature is capable of receiving it as God's gift; if it is not capable of it, then it is not capable of happiness either. For a man to live happily, after all, he must live. How can the happy life remain with him if life itself forsakes him as he dies? When it does forsake him, he is without doubt either unwilling for it to do so, or willing, or neither. If he is unwilling, how is this life happy which is in his will without being in his power? If no one is happy by wanting something and not having it, how much less than happy must he be who is being forsaken against his will not by honour, or possessions, or anything else, but by the happy life itself, when he comes to have no life at all?

So even if he has no senses left to be unhappy with (the reason the happy life is leaving him is that all life is leaving him), still, as long as he is conscious, he is unhappy because he knows that he is losing against his will what he loves more that anything else, and what he loves anything else for. So life cannot both be happy and forsake a man against his will, because no one is made happy against his will; thus it would make him unhappy if he had it against his will, so how much more will it do so when it forsakes him against his will? If however, it is in accordance with his will that it forsakes him, then how can this life have been a happy one that the man who had it wanted to lose?

The only thing left for them to say is that the happy man is conscious of neither attitude; that is, he is neither willing nor unwilling to be forsaken by the happy life when all life forsakes him at death, because he takes up his position between the two attitudes with a steady equanimity. But then his life can scarcely be the happy one if it does not merit the love of the man it is supposed to make happy. How can the life be happy which the happy man does not love? And how can he really love it if he does not care whether it flourishes or perishes? Unless perhaps the very virtues which we only love for the sake of happiness would dare to persuade us not to love happiness itself. If they do this, then we stop loving them too, when we no longer love the happiness for whose sake alone we loved the virtues.

In any case, what will become of the truth of this axiom, so tried, so tested, so clarified – that all men want to be happy – if those who are already happy are neither willing nor unwilling to be so? If they want it, as the truth cries out that they do and as nature compels them to, having this will implanted in it by the supremely good and unchangeably happy creator, if those who are happy do want to be happy, I say, then of course they do not want not to be happy. And if they do not want not to be happy, then without a doubt they do not want their being happy to fade away and cease. They cannot be happy unless they are alive; therefore they do not want their being alive to cease.

So any one who is truly happy or desires to be, wants to be immortal. But a man does not live happily if he has not got what he wants; so it is altogether impossible for a life to be genuinely happy unless it is immortal. Whether human nature is capable of something it confesses to be so desirable is no small question. But if the faith possessed by those to whom Jesus 'gave the right to become sons of God' (John 1:12) is to hand, then there is no question at all.

People have tried to work these things out by human reasoning, but it is the immortality of the soul alone that they have succeeded in getting to some notion of, and then only a few of them, and with difficulty, and only if they have had plenty of brains and plenty of leisure and plenty of education in abstruse learning.

Even so, they never discovered a lasting, which is to say a true, life of happiness for this soul. They actually said it returned to the unhappiness of this life after happiness. Some of them, it is true, were ashamed of such an opinion, and thought that the purified soul should be placed in everlasting happiness without the body; yet they have had views about the eternity of the world backward in time that simply contradict this opinion of theirs about the soul. It would take too long to prove this here, but in any case I have sufficiently explained it, I think, in the twelfth book of *The City of God*.

This faith of ours, however, promises on the strength of divine authority, not of human argument, that the whole man, who consists of course of soul and body too, is going to be immortal, and therefore truly happy. That is why in the Gospel it did not just stop when it had said that Jesus 'gave those who received him the right to become sons of God', and briefly explained what receiving him meant by saying 'to those who believe in his name', and then had shown how they would become sons of God by adding that they 'are born not of blood nor of the will of the flesh nor of the will of the man, but of God' (John 1:12). But in case this feebleness that is man, which we see and carry around with us, should despair of attaining such eminence, it went on to say 'And the Word became flesh and dwelt amongst us' (John 1:14), in order to convince us of what might seem incredible by showing us its opposite.

For surely if the Son of God by nature became son of man by mercy for the sake of the sons of men (that is the meaning of 'the Word became flesh and dwelt amongst us'), how much easier it is to believe that the sons of men by nature can become sons of God by grace and dwell in God; for it is in him alone and thanks to him alone that they can be happy, by sharing in his immortality; it was to persuade us of this that the Son of God came to share in our mortality.

Grassy meadows
Prudentius

Prudentius (348–405) was a Latin Christian poet who lived in the region round Tarragona in Spain. He practised law, acted as a provincial governor, and eventually retired to live a life of fasting and prayer. This lyric is in the translation of Helen Waddell.

Easter Eve

>   The earth is sweet with roses,
>   And rich with marigold,
>   And violets and crocus
>   Are wet with running streams ...
>
>   And through the grassy meadows,
>   The blessed spirits go,

129

Their white feet shod with lilies,
And as they go they sing.

Get nearer the sun
Richard Baxter

Richard Baxter (1615–91), who could not accept episcopal church order, acted as a minister at Kidderminster, Worcestershire, from 1641 until the Act of Uniformity in 1662 deprived him of his living. During the next 25 years he was several times in trouble with the law for holding meetings for worship in London, being imprisoned by Judge Jeffreys for two years in 1685. The Act of Indulgence of 1687 eased things for him, and he lived peacefully, preaching and writing. He had great influence in America. The passage here comes from The Saints' Everlasting Rest *(1650).*

Once more consider, God seldom gives his people so sweet a foretaste of their future rest as in their deep afflictions. He keeps his most precious cordials for the time of our greatest faintings and dangers. He gives them when he knows they are needed and will be valued; and when he is sure to be thanked for them, and his people rejoiced by him. Especially when our sufferings are more directly for his cause, then he seldom fails to sweeten the bitter cup.

The martyrs have possessed the highest joys. When did Christ preach such comfort to his disciples as when their hearts were sorrowful at his departure? When did he appear among them, and say, 'Peace be unto you', but when they were shut up for fear of the Jews? When did Stephen see heaven opened, but when he was giving up his life for the testimony of Jesus? Is not that our best state wherein we have most of God? Why else do we desire to come to heaven? If we look for a heaven of fleshy delights we shall find ourselves mistaken.

Conclude then that affliction is not so bad a state for a saint in his way to rest. Are we wiser than God? Doth he not know what is good for us as well as we? Or is he not as careful of our good as we are of our own? Woe to us, if he were not much more so and if he did not love us better than we love either him or ourselves!

Say not, 'I could bear any other affliction but this.' If God had afflicted thee where thou canst bear it, thy idol would neither have been discovered nor removed. Neither say, 'If God would deliver me out of it, I could be content to bear it.' Is it nothing that he hath promised it shall work for thy good? Is it not enough that thou art sure to be delivered at death? Nor let it be said, 'If my affliction did not disable me for duty, I could bear it.' It doth not disable thee for that duty which tendeth to thy own personal benefit, but is the greatest quickening help thou canst expect. As for the duty to others, it is not thy duty when God disables thee.

Perhaps thou wilt say, 'The godly are my afflictors; if it were ungodly men, I could easily bear it.' Whoever is the instrument, the affliction is from God, and the deserving cause thyself; and is it not better to look more to God and thyself? Didst thou not know that the best men are sinful in part? Do not plead, 'If I had but that consolation which you say God reserveth for suffering times, I should suffer more contentedly; but I do not perceive any such thing.' The more you suffer for righteousness' sake, the more of this blessing you may expect; and the more you suffer for your own evil doings the longer it will be before that sweetness comes. Are not the comforts you desire, neglected or resisted? Have your afflictions wrought kindly with you, and fitted you for comfort? It is not mere suffering that prepares you for comfort, but the success and fruit of sufferings upon your heart.

A heavenly mind is the nearest and truest way to a life of comfort. The countries far north are cold and frozen because they are distant from the sun. What makes such frozen uncomfortable Christians but their living so far from heaven? And what makes others so warm in comforts but their living higher and having nearer access to God?

When the sun in the spring draws our part of the earth, how do all things congratulate its approach? The earth looks green; the trees shoot forth, the plants revive, the birds sing, and all things smile upon us. If we would but try this life with God and keep these hearts above, what a spring of joy would be within us? How should we forget our winter sorrows? How early should we rise to sing the praises of our great Creator?

O Christian, get above. Those that have been there, have found it warmer, and I doubt not but thou hast sometime tried it thyself. When have your largest comforts? Is it not when thou hast conversed with God, and talketh with the inhabitants of the higher world, and viewed their mansions and filled thy soul with the forethoughts of glory? If thou knowest by experience what this practice is I dare say thou knowest what spiritual joy is.

If, as David professes, the light of God's countenance more gladdens the heart than corn and wine then, surely, they that draw near it, and most behold it, must be fullest of these joys. Whom should we blame then, that we are so void of consolation, but our own negligent hearts? God hath provided us a crown of glory, and promised to set it shortly on our heads, and we will not so much as think of it. He bids us behold and rejoice, and we will not so much as look at it and yet we complain for want of comfort. It is by believing that we are filled with joy and peace, and no longer than we continue our believing. It is in hope that the saints rejoice, and no longer than they continue hoping.

God's Spirit worketh our comforts, by setting our own spirits on work upon the promises, and raising our thoughts to the place of our comforts. As you would delight a covetous man by shewing him gold so God delights his people by leading them, as it were, into heaven, and shewing them himself and their rest with him. He does not cast in our joys while we are idle, or taken up with other things. He gives the fruits of the earth while we plow and sow, and weed, and water, and dung, and dress, and with patience expect his blessing; so doth he give the joys of the soul.

I intreat thee, Reader, in the name of the Lord, and as thou valuest the life of constant joy, and that good conscience, which is a continual feast, to set upon this work seriously, and learn the art of heavenly mindedness, and thou shalt find the increase a hundredfold, and the benefit abundantly exceed thy labour. But this is the

132

misery of man's nature; though every man naturally hates sorrow, and loves the most merry and joyful life, yet few live the way to joy, or will endure the pains by which it is obtained; they will take the next that comes to hand, and content themselves with earthly pleasures, rather than they will ascend to heaven to seek it; and yet when all is done, they must have it there, or be without it.

Hungerly to a pilchard
John Mabbe

John Mabbe (1582–1642) was a Spanish scholar and a fellow of Magdalen College, Oxford. A pseudonym he used was Don Diego Puede-Ser ('May-Be', a play on his name). He translated some picaresque tales and Cervantes' Exemplary Novels. He gave his own interpretation to a series of sermons on the Gospels of Lent by Cristobal de Fonseca when he published them in Englsh in 1629 under the title Devout Contemplations.

'Man shall not live by bread alone.' S. Chrysostom, touching the care & provision that ought to bee had of things necessarie for this life, sayth that it is not so convenient a meanes to seeke after the aboundance of things, as to have God to our friend; wherein he recommendeth unto us the wonderfull care of God's divine providence for our good, howbeit by the world ill understood & worse executed. Whereas indeed wee should consider with our selves, that the end of our sweates and our labours being to enjoy some sweetnesse and content in this life, they injoy it most and most safely who injoy least of the pleasures of this life.

For they that abound in Riches abound in Cares, and Wealth is the mother of Woe. The Princes of this world, and your great powerfull men, have more gold than gylding in their beds, but yet they have no golden sleepes; their braines have too much Quickesilver in them to settle to any rest. They have their fat Capons and their daintie Pheasants set before them in vessels of silver, but they have Leaden stomackes, and have no appetite to eate. Whereas your husbandman sleepes betweene furrow and furrow, and that soundly, having a clod of earth for his pillow, and fals as hungerly to a Pilchard and a clove of Garlicke as if hee had all the choice dishes in the world. For, Non in solo pane vivit homo.

The Children of Israel beeing thirtie yeares in the Wildernesse, God drew water for them out of the Rocke, and it seemed sweeter unto them than Honey, that is, De petra melle saturavit eos. It is a great comfort to a man, to have a God that is able to make us to be better contented with hunger than with all the dainties and curious fare that the world or sea can affoord.

Esay [Isaiah] pondring with himselfe how richly & how happily a man doth live under the shadow of God's wing, and his divine protection, saith 'It is above all Glorie'. The Prophet there treateth of those great favours which God shewed to his People; as that Piller which served them in the night as a Torch and was as a Tent pitcht about them in the day time; that priviledge which he gave them that neither the gravell nor the sand should weare out their shooes, nor time nor the bushes in the Deserts wast their cloathes: making this in the end (as it were) a burthen of his Song, Super omnem gloriam protectio. Great were all those glories which that People did enjoy; but above all was God's blessed protection towards them. The rich and mightie men of this world enjoy much in this life; but I had rather o Lord, bee poore. Sub tegmine alarum tuarum, Under the covering of thy wings.

Give me the scorpions
William Habington

William Habington (1605–54) conjures up a series of extravagant horrors he would rather suffer than go to hell.

> Fix me on some bleake precipice,
> Where I ten thousand yeares may stand;
> Made now a statue of ice,
> Then by the sommer scorcht and tan'd!

Place me alone in some fraile boate
'Mid th' horrors of an angry Sea:
Where I while time shall live, may floate
Despairing either land or day!

Or under earth my youth confine
To th' night and silence of a cell:
Where Scorpions may my limbes entwine.
O God! So thou forgive me hell.

Forget servile fear
Augustine Baker

*Augustine Baker (1575–1641) was a lawyer in London who became a Bene-
dictine monk, a choice that obliged him in those days to live abroad. The spiritual advice that he compiled when a chaplain to English nuns at Cambrai was
edited after his death by Serenus Cressy and published as* Sancta Sophia *in
1657. It became a spiritual classic. In the passage below he deals with the
thought that worries many people: What's to become of me when I'm dead?*

As for the inward and painful subject of fear – which is the uncertainty of a future eternal condition after death, which doth usually
much afflict and deject imperfect souls that are conscious of their
manifold defects, small satisfaction paid for them, great weakness
of divine love (a proof whereof is this very fear, which would be
expelled if charity were perfect) – it is a hard matter to encourage
such souls against it, or to persuade them to mortify it and resign
themselves willingly to support it, it being indeed very profitable
and healthful to the soul. On the contrary, they think resignation
in this case to be scarce a fitting or lawful thing, though most certainly it is so.

I do not say that such souls ought to bring themselves to an indifference what way they shall be disposed of after death. But the point
of resignation lies in this, that a soul ought to content herself not to

know how and in what manner God will dispose of her after death. Her anchor is hope, which she ought to cherish and fortify all she can, and the best way for souls to fortify that is to make as few reflections on themselves as may be, and to employ all their thoughts and affections directly upon God.

It is divine love alone that is at least the principal virtue that brings souls to beatitude, and therefore fearful souls, though they were in as dangerous a state as they suspect, must needs rationally argue thus: that the way to procure and strengthen love is by fixing their minds upon the mercies, goodness, and perfections of God, and to contradict or forget all arguments or motives of servile fear, the greatest enemy of love.

What folly is it, because they are imperfect, therefore wilfully to continue in their imperfections by nourishing fear! Surely, at the close of our lives we ought to practise after the best manner we can the best actions, and most acceptable to God, which is to relinquish ourselves, and to contemplate, trust, rely, and roll ourselves upon him.

Let the afflicted soul, therefore, herein as in all other matters, not only with patience support such an ignorance, but with an amorous resignation congratulate with God his eternal most secret purposes and decrees concerning her, both for time and eternity, freely consenting and agreeing to the will of God that such secrets should be reserved to His own breast, hidden from our knowledge, therein acknowledging his divine wisdom and goodness, which moved him (doubtless for our good) to conceal from us those things the knowledge of which would have bred security, negligence, and perhaps pride, in our corrupt hearts. Let her desire be to know nothing, and to have nothing but what, when, and in what manner it doth please Almighty God.

Such behaviour of hers towards her Creator and Redeemer (to whom she belongs both for her being and manner of it), as it is most just and reasonable, so it will make her most acceptable to God, and in conclusion, most assuredly bring her to happiness; whereas to be dejected and disquieted because God will not reveal His secret purposes to her is most unreasonable, and can proceed from no other ground but natural pride and self-love. And to give a deliberate scope to unquietness so grounded is both dishonourable to God and utterly useless to the soul herself; for assuredly God will not, to satisfy the inordinate desires of nature, alter the course of His divine providence.

It did not hinder or abate the tranquillity of Adam's state in innocence that he was uncertain of perseverance, yea, though he knew that one sin committed would exclude him utterly from his present happiness; whereas, in our present state, after thousands of sins, one act of true conversion to God and amorous resignation to his will is able to restore us.

Let the soul withal consider that he which hath denied unto her an assurance and forbidden her to presume, hath yet commanded her to hope, and to comfort herself in that hope. Let her therefore frequently and seriously exercise acts of hope (how little gust so-ever sensuality finds in them; for the greater repugnance there is in inferior nature, the more generous are such acts and more acceptable to God), which acts are to be grounded not upon any conceits of our own innocency or worth; for if the soul were never so perfect, yet a conceit of her own innocency would be but a rotten foundation of hope, which should regard only the free mercies of God, the merits of his Son, etc.

Moreover, let her exercise these acts, not as acts of her own will, but (far more perfectly and divinely) as acts of God's own will, who hath commanded us thus to hope. She may withal, if need be, make use of considerations and motives in the understanding, by reading or hearing comfortable promises in Scripture etc., to incline the will to conform itself to the divine will; to which conformity when a soul shall once perfectly be brought, there remains to her no hell nor purgatory, no more than to God himself; for where there is no propriety of will there is nothing but the divine will, which is God himself, and according to the measure of this conformity such will be the measure of our happiness.

Trust
Emily Dickinson

Emily Dickinson (1830–86) lived quietly, later reclusively, at Amherst, Massachusetts. Only ten of her poems were published in her lifetime, but she left more than 1700 bound up in booklets. The one here was first printed in Unpublished Poems *(1935).*

Trust in the Unexpected –
By this – was William Kidd
Persuaded of the Buried Gold –
As One had testified –

Through this – the old Philosopher –
His Talismanic Stone
Discerned – still withholden
To effort undivine –

'Twas this – allured Colombus –
When Genoa – withdrew
Before an Apparition
Baptized America –

The Same – afflicted Thomas –
When Deity assured
'Twas better – the perceiving not –
Provided it believed –

God with us

Sweet concord
Boethius

*Boethius (480–525), a Christian who was executed by the violent and hetero-
dox Ostrogoth king Theodoric, wrote while awaiting death his* Consolation
of Philosophy, *a book translated into English by Alfred the Great, by Chaucer
and by Queen Elizabeth, who added to it some obscurities of her own. Boethius's
philosophy detects the providence of God ruling all things. In the metrical passage below, by the 'law of kindness' is meant the natural affinity some things
have for others — heat tempers cold and humidity dryness; fire flies up, earth
falls by gravity to the centre. It is part of what Dante later meant by 'the love
that rules the sun and the other stars'. These are divinely implanted laws. The
translation is by Henry Vaughan (1621–95).*

Who would unclouded see the Laws
Of the supreme, eternal Cause,
Let him with careful thoughts and eyes
Observe the high and spatious Skyes.
There in one league of Love the Stars
Keep their old peace, and shew our wars.
The Sun, though flaming still and hot,
The cold, pale Moon annoyeth not.
Arcturus with his Sons (though they
See other stars go a far way,
And out of sight), yet still are found
Near the North pole, their noted bound.
Bright Hesper (at set times) delights
To usher in the dusky nights:
And in the East again attends
To warn us, when the day ascends,

So alternate Love supplys
Eternal Courses still, and vies
Mutual kindness; that no jars
Nor discord can disturb the Stars.
The same sweet Concord here below
Makes the fierce Elements to flow
And Circle without quarrel still,
Though temper'd diversly; thus will
The Hot assist the Cold; the Dry
Is a friend to Humidity.
And by the Law of kindness they
The like relief to them repay.
The fire, which active is and bright,
Tends upward, and from thence gives light.
The Earth allows it all that space
And makes choice of the lower place;
For things of weight hast to the Centre
A fall to them is no adventure.
From these kind turns and Circulation
Seasons proceed and Generation.
This makes the Spring to yield us flow'rs,
And melts the Clouds to gentle show'rs.
The Summer thus matures all seeds
And ripens both the Corn and weeds.
This brings on Autumn, which recruits
Our old, spent store with new fresh fruits.
And the cold Winters blustring Season
Hath snow and storms for the same reason.
This temper and wise mixture breed
And bring forth ev'ry living seed.
And when their strength and substance spend
(For while they live, they drive and tend
Still to a change), it takes them hence
And shifts their dress; and to our sense
Their Course is over, as their birth:

And hid from us, they turn to Earth.
But all this while the Prince of life
Sits without loss, or change, or strife
Holding the Reins, by which all move
(And those his wisdom, power, Love
And justice are); and still what he
The first life bids, that needs must be,
And live on for a time; that done
He calls it back, meerly to shun
The mischief which his creature might
Run into by a further flight.
For if this dear and tender sense
Of his preventing providence
Did not restrain and call things back:
Both heav'n and earth would go to wrack.
And from their great preserver part,
As blood let out forsakes the Heart
And perisheth; but what returns
With fresh and Brighter spirits burns.
This is the Cause why ev'ry living
Creature affects an endless being.
A grain of this bright love each thing
Had giv'n at first by their great King;
And still they creep (drawn on by this);
And look back towards their first bliss.
For otherwise, it is most sure,
Nothing that liveth could endure:
Unless it's Love turn'd retrograde
Sought that first life, which all things made.

Snow in Salmon
John Spencer

John Spencer, the date of whose birth is unknown, was the librarian of Sion College in London and in 1658 published Things New and Old: Or, a Storehouse of Similes, Sentences, Allegories, Apophthegms, Adages, Apologues, Divine, Moral, Political, etc., *an astonishing collection of hundreds of anecdotes from ancient and modern history designed to illustrate aspects of Christian teaching.*

It is storyed of Andronicus, the old Emperour of Constantinople, that all things going crosse with him, he took a Psalter into his hand, to resolve his doubtfull mind, and opening the same, as it were of that divine Oracle to ask counsel, he lighted upon Psalme 68:14, 'When the Almighty scattered Kings, they shall be white as snow in Salmon', and was thereby comforted, and directed what to do for his better safety.

Now it is to be understood, that Salmon signifies 'shady and dark'. So was this Mount, by the reason of many lofty fair-spread Trees that were near it, but made lightsome by snow that covered it. Hence, to be white as snow in Salmon is to have joy in affliction, light in darknesse, mercy in the midst of judgement; as for instance, 'In sorrow shalt thou bring forth' (Genesis 3), saith God to the Woman; she shall have sorrow, but she shall bring forth – that's the comfort. Many are the troubles of the righteous – that's the sadnesse of their condition; but the Lord will deliver them out of them all – theres their rejoicing. There is no sorrow, no trouble, no temptation, that shall take any godly man, but he shall be as snow in Salmon; God will not suffer him to be tempted above that he is able, but will with the temptation also make a way to escape, that he may be able to bear it.

142

They flourished for me!
Thomas Traherne

*Thomas Traherne (1637–74) was an Anglican clergyman who gave his med-
itations and thanksgiving an extraordinary lyrical force. His reputation rested
posthumously on his* Serious and Pathetical Contemplation of the Mercies of God *(1699), from which the extract below from the 'Thanksgiving for
God's Providence' is taken. But his reputation has never been so high as in the
decades since 1896 when a series of chance discoveries brought to light first his*
Centuries, *a collection of meditations, and other writings, some found in a
manuscript on a burning rubbish dump in Lancashire in 1967. Not all his
work has yet been published. Traherne's view of salvation history is both
formal and personal.*

Thy Condescention in creating the Heavens
And the Earth,
Is wholly Wonderful!
Thy Bounty to Adam, To me in him,
Most Great and Infinite!
Blessed be thy Name for the Employment thou gavest him,
More Glorious than the World;
To see thy Goodness,
Contemplate thy Glory,
Rejoyce in thy Love,
Be Ravish'd with thy Riches,
Sing thy Praises,
Enjoy thy Works,
Delight in thy Highness,
Possess thy Treasures,
And much more Blessed be thy Holy Name,
For Restoring me by the Blood of Jesus,
To Thy glorious Works,
    Those blessed Employments.
It is my joy, O Lord, to see the Perfection of thy Love
    towards us in that Estate.

The Glory of thy Laws,
     Blessedness of thy Works,
     Highness of thine Image,
     Beauty of the Life that there was to be led
In Communion with Thee.
Those intended joys are mine, O Lord,
   In thee, my God, In Jesus Christ,
   In every Saint, In every Angel.
But the glorious Covenant, so graciously renewed!
O the Floods, the Seas, the Oceans,
Of Honey and Butter contained in it!
So many thousand Years since, my standing Treasure.
O teach me to Esteem it,
                    Reposite it in my Family;
As that, which by its Value, is made sacred,
Infinitely Sacred, because infinitely Blessed.
How ought our first Fathers
To have esteemed that Covenant!
To have laid it up for their Children's Children,
As the choicest Treasure,
The Magna Charta of Heaven and Earth,
By which they held their Blessedness;
The Evidence of their Nobility;
The antient Instrument of their League with God;
Their pledge & claim to eternal Glory;
The sacred Mystery of all their Peace!
But they Apostatized and provoked thy Displeasure,
Sixteen hundred and fifty six Years,
Till thou did'st send a Flood that swept them away:
Yet did'st thou give them
The Rite of Sacrificing
The Lamb of God.
To betoken his Death,
From the beginning of the World;
Shewedst them thy Glory;

And that of Immortality
By Enoch's Translation:
(Of which me also hast thou made the heir!)
In the midst of Judgments thou hadst mercy on Noah,
And saved'st us both
In an ARK by Water.
That Ark is mine,
Thy Goodness gave it me;
By preserving my Being and Felicity in it.
It more serveth me there where it is,
Than if all its Materials were now in my Fold.
In that Act did'st thou reveal thy Glory,
As much as by the Creation of the World it self;
Reveal thy Glory to me; and, by many such,
Dispel the foggs of Ignorance and Atheism,
That else would have benighted,
And drowned my Soul.
The Rainbow is a Seal,
Of thy renewed Covenant,
For which, to day, I praise thy Name.
As for the wicked
They revolted back from the Life of God,
But the holy Sages brightly shined:
Whom thy Goodness prepared,
To be the Light of the World,
Melchisedec, Noah, Abraham himself,
In whom thy Goodness Blessed Me thy Servant,
                              And all Nations.
Whom thy Goodness chiefly Blessed, by making a Blessing.
When the World would have extinguished Knowledge,
And have lost thy Covenant,
Thou heldest the Clew, and maintained'st my Lot,
And sufferedst not all to perish for ever.
Out of the Loins of thy beloved,
Thy Glory form'd a Kingdom for thy self,

Govern'd by Laws,
Made Famous by Miracles,
Exalted by Mercys,
Taught from Heaven.
In the Tabernacle of Witness, thou dwelledst among them.
Thy Servant David, in most Solemn Assemblies, sang
Thy Praises.
Thy Glory appeared in Solomon's Temple,
But more in his Wisdom;
And the Prosperity of thy People.
Thy Prophets, in their order, ministred to us.
The concealed Beauty of thy Ceremonies,
Is wholly mine.
To me they exhibit in the best of Hieroglyphicks,
JESUS CHRIST.
The Glory of their Ministery Service, and Expectation,
For two thousand Years, is my Enjoyment.
For my sake, and for thy Promise sake,
Did thy goodness forbear,
When their Sins had provoked Thee,
To destroy them wholly.
How did thy Goodness in the time of Distress,
Watch over them for Good!
When like a Spark in the Sea,
They were almost wholly Extinguished,
In the Babilonish Waves.
How, Lord, did'st thou Work, in that Night of Darkness!
Making thy Glory, and the Glory of Love,
More to appear:
Then was our Welfare turning upon the hinge,
Our Hope gasping for a little Life,
Our Glory brought to the pit's brink,
And beyond the possibility of human remedy,
Endangered in the Extinction of that Nation.

How then did thy Power shine!
In making Nehemiah the King's Cupbearer;
Hester Queen;
Mordecai a Prince;
The three Children cold in the furnace;
Daniel Lord chief President of 127 Provinces.
Zorobbabel and Ezra especial favorites;
And in sending thy people home,
Without any Ransom,
That the influence of thy promise
Might surely descend;
And our Saviour arise, out of David's Loins,
Be born at Bethlehem,
Crucified at Jerusalem,
According to the Prophesies, That went before concerning
    him.
Blessed Lord, I magnifie thy holy Name,
For his Incarnation;
For the Joy of the Angels that sang his praises;
        Star of his Birth;
        Wise men's Offerings that came from the East;
        Salutation of thy handmaid Mary;
        Ravishing Song of the blessed Virgin;
        Rapture and Inspiration of Zacharias thy Servant;
        Birth of John our Saviour's forerunner.
O Lord,
Who would have believed, that such a worm as I, should
have had such Treasures,
In thy celestial Kingdom!
In the Land Of Jury, 3000 miles from hence
So great a Friend! such a Temple!
Such a Brest-plate! Glittering with Stones of endless price!
Such Ephod! Mytre! Altar! Court! Priest! and Sacrifices!
All to shew me my Lord and Saviour.

By the Shining Light of nearer Ages,
    Universal consent of many Nations,
    Most powerful Light of thy blessed Gospel,
See that remoter in the Land of Jury,
More clearly to shine.
The universal Good which redounded to all,
Is poured upon me.
The root being beautified by all its branches,
The fountain enriched, and made famous by its streams;
Their Temple, Sacrifices, Oracles, Scriptures,
Ceremonies, Monuments of Antiquity
Miracles, Transactions, Hopes,
Have received credit, and magnificence;
   by successes,
By the Lustre, Authority and Glory,
    Conviction of Ages,
    Acknowledgment of Sages,
    Conversion of Philosophers,
Of Flourishing Cities, Empires,
Potentates, and mighty States.
All which enamel the Book of God,
And enrich it more for mine exaltation.
The very Trees and Fruits, and Fields, and Flowers, that did
   service unto them,
Flourished for me!
And here I live,
Praising thy Name!

New heart at dawn
Ambrose

Ambrose (340–97) was the capable public servant pressed by the people of Milan to become their bishop. Augustine of Hippo went to him to seal his conversion. Ambrose's tact and courage were matched by his devotion, which he

148

instilled in the people by composing sacred hymns that they could sing to keep their spirits up. The one below, translated by Helen Waddell, connects cosmic providence with the personal contrition of the Apostles' leader, St Peter.

Eternal, Thou
Didst earth's foundations lay,
Dost rule the night and day,
And givest a time
That those whom time hath wearied may have rest.

The cock,
The clarion of the day,
Who keeps his vigil at the dead of night,
To wayfarers a light,
Now sings his lay,
Dividing night from night.

He wakes the Morning Star
That clears away the dark,
And all the company
Of wandering souls
Are off their evil road.

And at that sound
The sailor takes new heart,
The sea grows gentle.
The cock crew and
Peter, Rock of the Church,
Wept out his sin.

Faith without a hope
G.K. Chesterton

Chesterton (1872–1936) was the author in his 'Ballad of the White Horse' of that memorable phrase 'naught for your comfort'. The long poem is very readable still, and, if one has to allow that it follows the style of the late 19th century, it remains full of insights into false idols and fears. It also expresses an ancient virtue that really existed, a Christianized heroic ideal. It is the same bravery in the face of apparent disaster that the men led by the historical Byrhtnoth showed as they fell beside him, resisting the heathen Vikings at the Battle of Maldon in 991: 'Hige sceal the heardra, heorte the cenre / mod sceal the mare, the ure maegen lytlath' — Courage must be firmer, heart the braver / More proud the spirit, as our strength lessens — as the Old English poem on that battle puts it. For them as for Chesterton's King Alfred it was better to die than to survive. And for Alfred 'faith without a hope' — hoping beyond hope — brought him to victory alive.

The Northmen came about our land
A Christless chivalry:
Who knew not of the arch, or pen,
Great, beautiful half-witted men
From the sunrise and the sea.

Misshapen ships stood on the deep
Full of strange gold and fire,
And hairy men, as huge as sin
With horned heads, came wading in
Through the long, low sea-mire.

Our towns were shaken of tall kings
With scarlet beards like blood:
The world turned empty where they trod,
They took the kindly cross of God
And cut it up for wood.

Their souls were drifting as the sea.
And all good towns and lands
They only saw with heavy eyes,
And broke with heavy hands.

Their gods were sadder than the sea,
Gods of a wandering will,
Who cried for blood like beasts at night,
Sadly, from hill to hill.

They seemed as trees walking the earth,
As witless and as tall,
Yet they took hold upon the heavens
And no help came at all.

They bred like birds in English woods,
They rooted like the rose,
When Alfred came to Athelney
To hide him from their bows

There was not English armour left,
Nor any English thing,
When Alfred came to Athelney
To be an English king.

For earthquake swallowing earthquake
Uprent the Wessex tree;
The whirlpool of the pagan sway
Had swirled his sires as sticks away
When a flood smites the sea.

And the great kings of Wessex
Wearied and sank in gore,
And even their ghosts in that great stress
Grew greyer and greyer, less and less,
With the lords that died in Lyonesse
And the king that comes no more.

And the God of the Golden Dragon
Was dumb upon his throne,
And the lord of the Golden Dragon
Ran in the woods alone.

And if ever he climbed the crest of luck
And set the flag before,
Returning as a wheel returns,
Came ruin and the rain that burns,
And all began once more.

And naught was left King Alfred
But shameful tears of rage,
In the island in the river
In the end of all his age.

In the island in the river
He was broken to his knee:
And he read, writ with an iron pen,
That God had wearied of Wessex men
And given their country, field and fen,
To the devils of the sea.

And he saw in a little picture,
Tiny and far away,
His mother sitting in Egbert's hall,
And a book she showed him, very small,
Where a sapphire Mary sat in stall
With a golden Christ at play.

It was wrought in the monk's slow manner,
From silver and sanguine shell,
Where the scenes are little and terrible,
Keyholes of heaven and hell.

In the river island of Athelney,
With the river running past,
In colours of such simple creed
All things sprang at him; sun and weed,
Till the grass grew to be grass indeed
And the tree was a tree at last.

Fearfully plain the flowers grew,
Like the child's book to read,
Or like a friend's face seen in a glass;
He looked; and there Our Lady was,
She stood and stroked the tall live grass
As a man strokes his steed.

Her face was like an open word
When brave men speak and choose,
The very colours of her coat
Were better than good news.

She spoke not, nor turned not,
Nor any sign she cast,
Only she stood up straight and free,
Between the flowers in Athelney,
And the river running past.

One dim ancestral jewel hung
On his ruined armour grey,
He rent and cast it at her feet:
Where, after centuries, with slow feet,
Men came from hall and school and street
And found it where it lay.

'Mother of God,' the wanderer said,
'I am but a common king,
Nor will I ask what saints may ask,
To see a secret thing.

'The gates of heaven are fearful gates
Worse than the gates of hell;
Not I would break the splendours barred
Or seek to know the thing they guard,
Which is too good to tell.

'But for this earth most pitiful,
This little land I know,
If that which is for ever is,
Or if our hearts shall break with bliss,
Seeing the stranger go?

'When our last bow is broken, Queen,
And our last javelin cast,
Under some sad, green evening sky,
Holding a ruined cross on high,
Under warm westland grass to lie,
Shall we come home at last?'

And a voice came human but high up,
Like a cottage climbed among
The clouds; or a serf of hut and croft
That sits by his hovel fire as oft,
But hears on his old bare roof aloft
A belfry burst in song.

'The gates of heaven are lightly locked
We do not guard our gain,
The heaviest hind may easily
Come silently and suddenly
Upon me in a lane.

'And any little maid that walks
In good thoughts apart,
May break the guard of the Three Kings
And see the dear and dreadful things
I hid within my heart.

'The meanest man in grey fields gone
Behind the set of sun,

Heareth between star and other star,
Through the door of the darkness fallen ajar
The council, eldest of things that are,
The talk of the Three in One.

'The gates of heaven are lightly locked,
We do not guard our gold,
Men may uproot where worlds begin,
Or read the name of the nameless sin;
But if he fail or if he win
To no good man is told.

'The men of the East may spell the stars,
And times and triumphs mark,
But the men signed of the cross of Christ
Go gaily in the dark.

'The men of the East may search the scrolls
For sure fates and fame,
But the men that drink the blood of God
Go singing to their shame.

'The wise men know what wicked things
Are written on the sky,
They trim sad lamps, they touch sad strings,
Hearing the heavy purple wings,
Where the forgotten seraph kings
Still plot how God shall die.

'The wise men know all evil things
Under the twisted trees,
Where the perverse in pleasure pine
And men are weary of green wine
And sick of crimson seas.

'But you and all the kind of Christ
Are ignorant and brave,
And you have wars you hardly win
And souls you hardly save.

'I tell you naught for your comfort,
Yea, naught for your desire,
Save that the sky grows darker yet
And the sea rises higher.

'Night shall be thrice night over you,
And heaven an iron cope.
Do you have joy without a cause,
Yea, faith without a hope?'

Even as she spoke she was not,
Nor any word said he,
He only heard, still as he stood
Under the old night's nodding hood,
The sea-folk breaking down the wood
Like a high tide from sea.

He only heard the heathen men,
Whose eyes are blue and bleak,
Singing about some cruel thing
Done by a great and smiling king
In daylight on a deck.

He only heard the heathen men,
Whose eyes are blue and blind,
Singing what shameful things are done
Between the sunlit sea and the sun
When the land is left behind.

Our Captain God
Bede

Bede (673–735) lived in monastic peace when the coasts of the north country in which he lived were racked with raids by Vikings. He set no store by swords of iron, but made his prayer, here translated by Helen Waddell, for a sword of the spirit to cut down the invisible dragon of wickedness.

O God that art the only hope of the world,
The only refuge for unhappy men,
Abiding in the faithfulness of heaven,
Give me strong succour in this testing place.
O King, protect thy man from utter ruin
Lest the weak faith surrender to the tyrant,
Facing innumerable blows alone.
Remember I am dust, and wind, and shadow,
And life as fleeting as the flower of grass.
But may the eternal mercy which hath shone
From time of old
Rescue thy servant from the jaws of the lion.
Thou who didst come from on high in the cloak of flesh,
Strike down the dragon with that two-edged sword
Whereby our mortal flesh can war with the winds
And beat down strongholds, with our Captain God.

Jesus

The best friend
Thomas à Kempis

Thomas à Kempis (1380–1471) was schooled at Deventer, now in the Nether-
lands, by the Brothers of the Common Life, who lived in a community without
vows and were at that time much influenced by the 'new devotion', a spirituality
which sought to return to the fervour of the first Christians. Thomas then became
a Canon Regular of St Augustine, in which vocation he lived a long life. His
authorship of The Imitation of Christ *has been questioned, but he is the*
most obvious candidate, and would certainly have approved of its concentration
on closeness to Jesus Christ. Ever since it was written the Imitation *has been*
popular in English-speaking countries, among Christians of various traditions.
The translation below was made by John Wesley.

1. When Jesus is present, all is well, and nothing seemeth difficult;
    but when Jesus is absent, every thing is hard.
      When Jesus speaketh not inwardly, we have no true comfort;
    but if Jesus speak but one word, we feel much consolation.
      Did not Mary presently rise from the place where she wept,
    when Martha said unto her, 'The Master is come, and calleth
    for thee'?
      Happy the hour when Jesus calleth from tears to spiritual joy.
      How dry and cold art thou without Jesus! how foolish and
    vain, if thou desire any thing out of Jesus!
      Is not this a greater loss, than if thou shouldst lose the whole
    world?
2. What can the world profit thee without Jesus?
    To be without Jesus is a grievous hell, and to be with Jesus a
    sweet paradise.
    If Jesus be with thee, no enemy can hurt thee.

He that findeth Jesus, findeth a good treasure, yea a good above all goods:

And he that loseth Jesus, loseth too much, and more than the whole world.

He is most poor, that liveth without Jesus: and he is most rich, that is well with Jesus.

3. It is a great skill to know to converse with Jesus, and great wisdom to know to keep Jesus.

Be humble and peaceable, and Jesus will be with thee.

Be devout and quiet, and Jesus will stay with thee.

Thou mayest soon drive away Jesus and lose his grace, if thou turn aside to outward things.

And if thou shouldst drive him away, and lose him; unto whom wilt thou fly, and what friend wilt thou seek?

Without a friend thou canst not live well: and if Jesus be not above all friends unto thee, thou shalt be very sorrowful and desolate.

Thou doest therefore foolishly, if thou dost trust or rejoice in any other.

It is better for thee to have all the world against thee, than Jesus offended with thee.

Of all things that are dear to thee therefore, let Jesus alone be peculiarly thy beloved.

4. Love all for Jesus, but Jesus for himself.

Jesus Christ alone is singularly to be beloved, who alone is good and faithful above all friends.

For him, and in him, let as well friends as foes be dear unto thee, and thou art to pray to him for all these, that all may know and love him.

Never desire to be singularly commended or beloved, for that appertaineth only unto God, who hath none like unto himself.

Neither do thou desire that the heart of any should be set on thee, nor do thou set thy heart on any: but let Jesus be in thee, and in every good man.

5. Be pure and free within, and entangle not thy heart with any creature.

Thou must be naked, and carry a pure heart to God, if thou wouldst be at liberty to see how sweet the Lord is.

And truly, unless thou be prevented and drawn by his grace, thou shalt never attain to this, to forsake and cast off all, that thou alone mayest be united to him alone.

For when the grace of God cometh unto a man, then he has power to do all things. And when that retires, he is poor and weak, and as it were left only to affliction.

In this thou oughtest not to be dejected, nor despair; but to resign thyself with all indifferency unto the will of God, and to bear all things that befall thee for the glory of Christ: for after winter followeth summer, after night cometh day, and after a storm a great calm.

The lamb came to me
Francis Kilvert

Francis Kilvert (1840–79) recorded in his diary an old woman's memories relating to the parable of the lost sheep (Matthew 18:10).

Thursday, 24 August, St Bartholomew's Day, 1871 After breakfast I went to read to old Caroline Farmer. Little Carrie was with her and opened the door to me with a brilliant smile. The child was taking care of her grandmother. I brought them some apricots. Carrie had never seen an apricot before and did not know what they were. She ate one and wrapped one carefully up in the apricot leaves to take home for her mother at one o'clock when she went home to dinner.

I began to read to Caroline the parable of the lost sheep. Suddenly the old woman laid her hand on my arm and said earnestly and impressively: 'When I was seven years old, about as big as Carrie, there I was keeping sheep on Locke's Heath near Spy Park.

One Sunday night I lost a lamb. I left the rest of the sheep and wandered about for three days looking for the lamb. I found him on
Thursday morning. He was tired and hungry and he was eating
briar leaves. There was a shepherd near the place where I found
him, folding a flock of sheep on turnips. The lamb would not join
the flock nor eat the turnips. The shepherd said I should not have
the lamb unless he would come to me by calling. So I called the
lamb and he came to me. I was very glad to see him again. If I had
not found him, Father must have paid the farmer for his loss. I took
off my pinafore and put it round the lamb's neck and so led him
home. I was more anxious about that lamb than about all the rest.'

Know, love and follow
Richard of Chichester

*Richard of Chichester (1197–1253) was made bishop of the cathedral from
which he derives his surname in 1245. The king of England opposed the
appointment, but Richard calmly went about reforming his diocese and caring
for the poor.*

> O holy Jesus,
> merciful redeemer,
> friend and brother,
> may I know thee more clearly,
> love thee more dearly,
> and follow thee more nearly.

The secret garden
Francis de Sales

Francis de Sales (1567–1622) in his book The Love of God *declares that
God delights us. Francis often uses pleasant metaphors from natural history.
Here he makes his point through overlapping images: the soul as God's*

garden, which he enters, and where he then allows the soul to suckle, as a baby,
from God's breasts. The latter striking metaphor had been used by the English
mystic Julian of Norwich, though it is not likely that Francis would have read
her book. Francis also contemplates the breast as the closet or treasure-house of
the heavenly king, and likens milk to wine and wine to blood. The main images
are to be found in the Song of Solomon in the Bible — the garden, the apples, the
breasts, the wine, the milk — but here they are remixed. The translation from
Francis's French is the first made into English, published in 1630 by Miles Car
(1599–1674), a friend of the poet Richard Crashaw, who would have enjoyed
the boundless metaphysical conceits of this passage.

How by holy complacence we are made as little children, at our Saviour's breasts.

1. O God, how happie the soule is who takes pleasure in learning to
know that God is God, and that his bountie is an infinite bountie.
For this heavenly spouse, by this Gate of Complacence, enters into
her, and suppes with us, as we with him. We feede our selves with his
sweetnesse, by the pleasure which we take therein, and recollect our
heart, in the divine perfections, by repose we take therein: and this
repast is a supper by reason of the repose which doth follow it, complacence making us sweetely repose, in the deliciousnesse of the good
which delightes us, and wherwith we feede our heart.

2. 'Let my well-beloved come into his garden,' said the sacred
spouse, 'and let him eate therein the fruite of his apple-trees.' Now
the heavenly spouse comes into his garden when he comes into the
devote soule. For, seeing his delight is to be with the children of men,
where can he better lodge than in the countrie of the minde, which
he made to his likeness and similitude? He himselfe doth set in this
garden the loving complacence which we have in his bountie and
whereof we feede, as likewise his goodnesse doth take his repast
and repose in our complacence — so that againe our complacence is
augmented, to perceive that God is pleased to see us take pleasure in
him, in such sort that from these reciprocal pleasures the love of
incomparable complacence doth spring, by which our soule, being
made a garden of her spouse, and having from his bountie the

apple-trees of his delightes, she renders him the fruite thereof, being that he is pleased in the complacence she takes in him.

Thus doe we draw God's heart into ours, and he disperseth in it his precious balme. And thus is that practised which the holy Bride spoke with such joye: 'The king of my heart hath led me into his closet, we will exult and rejoyce in thee. Mindefull of thy breasts, more amiable than wine, the good doe love thee.' For I praye you, Theotime, what are the closets of this king of love, but his paps; which abounde in the varietie of sweetesse and delights. The breasts and dugs of the mother are the closet of the little infant's treasures. He hath no other riches then those, which are more precious unto him than gold, or the topaz, more beloved than the rest of the world.

3. The soule, then, which doth contemplate the infinite treasures of divine perfections in her well-beloved, holds her selfe too happie and rich, in that love doth make her mistress by complacence of all the perfections and contentments of her deare spouse. And even as the babie doth give little jerts towards his mother's pap, and hops with joye to see them discovered, and as the mother againe on her part doth present them unto him, with a love always a little for-wards: even so the devoute soule doth feele the dauncings and motions of an incomparable joye through the content which she hath in beholding the treasures of the perfections of the king of her holy love, but especially when she feels that he himselfe doth dis-cover them by love, and that amongst them that perfection of his infinite love doth excellently shine.

Hath not this faire soule reason to crie 'O my king, how amiable thy riches are, and how rich thy loves. Ah! which of us have more joye, thou that enjoyest it, or I who re-enjoye it? We daunce with mirth in memorie of thy breasts, and thy duggs, so plentifull in all excellencie of deliciousnesse. I, because my well-beloved doth enjoye it; thou because thy well-beloved doth re-enjoy it. For so we doe both enjoye it, since thy goodnesse makes thee enjoye my re-enjoying, and my love makes me re-enjoye thy enjoying. Ah! the just and the good doe love thee, and how can one be good and not love so great a goodnesse?'

163

Worldly princes keepe their treasures in the closets of their palaces, their armour in their castles. But the heavenly Prince keepes his treasures in his bosome; his armes within his breaste; and because his treasure is his goodnesse, as his weapons are his loves, his breaste and bosome resemble those of a tender mother, who hath two faire duggs, as two closets, rich with the sweetenesse of good milke, armed with as many darts to subdue her little deare babie as it makes shoots in sucking.

4. Nature surely lodged the duggs in the bosome, to th' end that, the heat of the heart concocting the milke, as the mother is the child's nourse, so her heart should be his foster-father, and that milke might be a foode of love, better a thousand times than wine. Note the while, Theotime, that the comparison of milke and wine seemes so proper to the holy spouse, that she is not content to have said once, that her spouse's breasts surpasseth wine, but she repeats it thrice.

Wine, Theotime, is the milke of grapes, and milke is the wine of the duggs: for so the sacred spouse saieth, that her well-beloved is to her a grape, but a Cyprine grape, that is, of as excellent odour. The Israelites, saieth Moyses, could drinke the purest and best blood of the grape, and Jacob describing unto his sonne Judas the share which they should have in the land of Promise, prophetizied under this figure the true felicitie of Christians, saying that our Saviour would wash his robe, that is, his holy Church, in the blood of the grape, that is, in his owne blood.

Now blood and milke are no more different than grapes and wine. For, as grapes ripening by the sun's heate, change their colour, become a gratefull and nourishing wine, so blood tempered by the heate of the heart, turns faire white, and, becomes a fit foode for children.

5. Milke which is a cordial foode wholly consisting of love, represents the mystical knowledge and divinitie, that is, the sweete relish which proceeds from the complacence of love which the minde receives in meditating the perfections of the divine Goodness. But wine signifies ordinarie and acquired knowledge, which is squeezed

by force of speculation from the presse of divers arguments and disputes. Now the milke which our soules draw from the breastes of our Saviour's charitie is incomparably better then the wine which we squeeze from humane discourse. For this milke floweth from heavenly love, which prepares it for his children, yea even before they yet thought of it. It hath a sweete and amiable gust, and the odour thereof puts downe all perfumes; it makes the breath pure and sweete, as of a sucking child. It gives joye, without insolencie; it inebriateth, without dulling. It doth not onely reare up, but doth even revive the senses.

6. When the holy man Isaac embraced and kissed his deare child Iacob, he smelt the good odour of his garments, and straight perfumed with an extreame pleasure. 'Oh,' quoth he, 'behold how the odour of my sonne is like to the odour of a flourishing field, which God bath blessed.' The garment and perfumes were upon Jacob, but Isaac had the complacence and re-enjoying of them. Ah, the soule which by love holds her Saviour in the armes of her affection, how deliciously doth she smell the perfumes of the infinite perfections which are found in him? With what complacence doth she say in herself, 'Behold how the scent of my God is like the smell of a flourishing garden, how precious are his breastes, sending out soveraigne parfumes?'

So the spirit of the great St Augustine, stayed in suspense betwixt the sacred contentments which he had to consider — on the one side the mysterie of his Maister's birth; on th'other that of the passion — cried out ravished in this complacence:

> Betwixt two sacred fires I burne,
> Nor know to which my heart to turne.
> From hence, a Mother doth present
> A fluent breast, a deare content:
> From thence, as from a Truest Vine
> Doth issue blood, in lieu of wine.

The fact itself
Anonymous

This short consideration comes from a card found between the pages of a prayer book.

The grace of Holy Communion is the fact itself. God comes, intimately, personally, with all His power and love, right down into the centre of our being where the springs of life and thought come up, and when He comes it is with healing and blessing and pacifying power, to put all in order, to make holy and strong and pure, what we so often drag down and wear out and misuse, our very soul and substance. So you see it is not a case of saying beautiful things to Him, of saying anything at all, but, all battered and wearied and dejected as we are, it is only a case of wanting and receiving Him, and the work is done without any words.

The Comforter

The shadow of thy wings
John Donne

John Donne (1572–1631) was a powerful poet of human love and a powerful preacher. He was learned, and informed his congregation, which they enjoyed. His English prose is a delight too, never stuck in obscurities but always urging on in energetic periods. In this, the third part of a sermon preached at St Paul's on January 29 1626, he explores the strength of God to console and save.

Psalm 63:7. Because thou hast been my helpe, therefore in the shadow of thy wings will I rejoyce.

First then, lest any man in his dejection of spirit, or of fortune, should stray into a jealousie or suspition of Gods power to deliver him, As God hath spangled the firmament with starres, so hath he his Scriptures with names, and Metaphors, and denotations of power. Sometimes he shines out in the name of a Sword, and of a Target, and of a Wall, and of a Tower, and of a Rocke, and of a Hill; And sometimes in that glorious and manifold constellation of all together, Dominus exercituum, 'The Lord of Hosts'. God, as God, is never represented to us, with Defensive Armes. He needs them not. When the Poets present their great Heroes, and their Worthies, they alwayes insist upon their Armes, they spend much of their invention upon the description of their Armes; both because the greatest valour and strength needs Armes, (Goliah himselfe was armed) and because to expose ones selfe to danger unarmed, is not valour, but rashnesse. But God is invulnerable in himselfe, and is never represented armed; you finde no shirts of mayle, no Helmets, no Cuirasses in Gods Armory. In that one place of Esay [Isaiah 59:17], where it may seeme to be otherwise where God is said to have 'put on

167

righteousnesse as a breastplate, and a Helmet of Salvation upon his head'; in that prophecy God is Christ, and is therefore in that place, called the Redeemer. Christ needed defensive armes, God does not. God's word does; His Scriptures doe; And therefore S. Hierome hath armed them, and set before every booke his Prologum galeatum, that prologue that armes and defends every booke from calumny. But though God need not, nor receive not defensive armes for himselfe, yet God is to us a Helmet, a Breastplate, a strong tower, a rocke, every thing that may give us assurance and defence; and as often as he will, he can refresh that Proclamation, Nolite tangere Christos meos, Our enemies shall not so much as touch us.

But here, by occasion of his Metaphore in this Text, (Sub umbra alarum, 'In the shadow of thy wings') we doe not so much consider an absolute immunity – That we shall not be touched – as a refreshing and consolation, when we are touched, though we be pinched and wounded. The Names of God, which are most frequent in the Scriptures, are these three, Elohim, and Adonai, and Iehovah; and to assure us of his Power to deliver us, two of these three are Names of Power. Elohim is Deus fortis, The mighty, The powerfull God: And (which deserves a particular consideration) Elohim is a plurall Name; It is not Deus fortis, but Dii fortes, powerfull Gods. God is all kinde of Gods; All kinds, which either Idolaters and Gentils can imagine (as Riches, or Justice, or Wisdome, or Valour, or such), and all kinds which God himself hath called gods, (as Princes, and Magistrates, and Prelates, and all that assist and helpe one another). God is Elohim, All these Gods, and all these in their height and best of their power; for Elohim, is Dii fortes, Gods in the plurall, and those plurall gods in their exaltation.

The second Name of God, is a Name of power too, Adonai. For, Adonai is Dominus, The Lord, such a Lord as is Lord and Proprietary of all his creatures, and all creatures are his creatures; And then, Dominium est potestas tum utendi, tum abutendi, sayes the law – To be absolute Lord of any thing, gives that Lord a power to doe what he will with that thing. God, as he is Adonai, The Lord, may give and take, quicken and kill, build and throw downe, where and whom he will. So then two of God's three Names are Names of absolute power, to imprint, and re-imprint an assurance in us, that hee can absolutely deliver us, and fully revenge us, if he will.

But then, his third Name, and that Name which hee chooses to himselfe, and in the signification of which Name, he employes Moses, for the reliefe of his people under Pharaoh, that Name Iehovah, is not a Name of Power, but onely of Essence, of Being, of Subsistence, and yet in the vertue of that Name, God relieved his people. And if, in my afflictions, God vouchsafe to visit mee in that Name, to preserve me in my being, in my subsistence in him, that I be not shaked out of him, disinherited in him, excommunicate from him, devested of him, annihilated towards him, let him, at his good pleasure, reserve his Elohim, and his Adonai, the exercises and declarations of his mighty Power, to those great publike causes that more concerne his Glory, than any thing that can befall me; But if he impart his Iehovah, enlarge himselfe so far towards me, as that I may live, and move, and have my beeing in him, though I be not instantly delivered, nor mine enemies absolutely destroyed, yet this is as much as I should promise my selfe, this is as much as the Holy Ghost intends in this Metaphor, Sub umbra alarum, 'Under the shadow of thy wings', that is a Refreshing, a Respiration, a Conservation, a Consolation in all afflictions that are indicted upon me.

Yet, is not this Metaphor of Wings without a denotation of Power. As no Act of God's, though it seeme to imply but spirituall comfort, is without a denotation of power, (for it is the power of God that comforts me; to overcome that sadnesse of soule, and that dejection of spirit, which the Adversary by temporall afflictions would induce upon me, is an act of his Power), so this Metaphor, 'The shadow of his wings', (which in this place expresses no more, than consolation and refreshing in misery, and not a powerfull deliverance out of it) is so often in the Scriptures made a denotation of Power too, as that we can doubt of no act of power, if we have this shadow of his wings.

169

For, in this Metaphor of Wings, doth the Holy Ghost expresse the Maritime power, the power of some Nations at Sea, in Navies, ('Woe to the land shadowing with wings'), that is, that hovers over the world, and intimidates it with her sailes and ships. In this Metaphor doth God remember his people, of his powerfull deliverance of them, ('You have seene what I did unto the Egyptians, and how I bare you on Eagle's wings, and brought you to my selfe.') In this Metaphor doth God threaten his and their enemies, what hee can doe, ('The noise of the wings of his Cherubims, are as the noise of great waters, and of an Army.')

So also, what hee will doe, ('Hee shall spread his wings over Bozrah, and at that day shall the hearts of the mighty men of Edom, be as the heart of a woman in her pangs.') So that, if I have the shadow of his wings, I have the earnest of the power of them too. If I have refreshing, and respiration from them, I am able to say, (as those three Confessors did to Nebuchadnessar) 'My God is able to deliver me,' I am sure he hath power; 'And my God will deliver me,' when it conduces to his glory, I know he will; 'But, if he doe not, bee it knowne unto thee, O King, we will not serve thy Gods'; Be it knowne unto thee, O Satan, how long soever God deferre my deliverance, I will not seeke false comforts, the miserable comforts of this world. I will not, for I need not; for I can subsist under this shadow of these Wings, though I have no more.

The Mercy-seat it selfe was covered with the Cherubims' Wings; and who would have more than Mercy? and a Mercyseat; that is, established, resident Mercy, permanent and perpetuall Mercy; present and familiar Mercy; a Mercy-seat. Our Saviour Christ intends as much as would have served their turne, if they had laid hold upon it, when hee sayes that hee 'would have gathered Ierusalem, as a henne gathers her chickens under her wings'.

And though the other Prophets doe (as ye have heard) mingle the signification of Power, and actuall deliverance, in this Metaphor of Wings, yet our Prophet, whom wee have now in especiall consideration, David, never doth so; but in every place where hee uses this Metaphor of Wings (which are in five or sixe severall Psalmes) still

170

hee rests and determines in that sense, which is his meaning here; That though God doe not actually deliver us, nor actually destroy our enemies, yet if hee refresh us in the shadow of his Wings, if he maintaine our subsistence (which is a religious Constancy) in him, this should not onely establish our patience, (for that is but halfe the worke) but it should also produce a joy, and rise to an exultation, which is our last circumstance. 'Therefore in the shadow of thy wings, I will rejoice.'

I would always raise your hearts, and dilate your hearts, to a holy joy, to a joy in the Holy Ghost. There may be a just feare, that men doe not grieve enough for their sinnes; but there may bee a just jealousie, and suspition too, that they may fall into inordinate griefe, and diffidence of God's mercy; And God hath reserved us to such times, as being the later times, give us even the dregs and lees of misery to drinke. For, God hath not onely let loose into the world a new spirituall disease; which is, an equality and an indifferency which religion our children, or our servants, or our companions professe; (I would not keepe company with a man that thought me a knave, or a traitor; with him that thought I loved not my Prince, or were a faithlesse man, not to be beleeved, I would not associate my selfe; And yet I will make him my bosome companion, that thinks I doe not love God, that thinks I cannot be saved). But God hath accompanied, and complicated almost all our bodily diseases of these times, with an extraordinary sadnesse, a predominant melancholy, a faintnesse of heart, a chearlesnesse, a joylesnesse of spirit, and therefore I returne often to this endeavor of raising your hearts, dilating your hearts with a holy Joy, Joy in the holy Ghost, for Under the shadow of his wings, you may, you should, rejoyce.

If you looke upon this world in a Map, you find two Hemisphears, two half worlds. If you crush heaven into a Map, you may find two Hemisphears too, two half heavens; halfe will be joy, and halfe will be Glory; for in these two, the joy of heaven, and the glory of heaven, is all heaven often represented unto us. And as of those two Hemisphears of the world, the first hath been knowne long before, but the other, (that of America, which is the richer in

171

treasure) God reserved for later Discoveries; so though he reserve
that Hemisphear of heaven, which is the Glory thereof, to the Resurrection, yet the other Hemisphear, the joy of heaven, God opens
to our Discovery, and delivers for our habitation even whilst we
dwell in this world.

As God hath cast upon the unrepentant sinner two deaths, a temporall, and a spirituall death, so hath he breathed into us two
lives; for so, as the word for death is doubled, Morte morieris, 'Thou
shalt die the death', so is the word for life expressed in the plural,
Chaiim, vitarum, 'God breathed into his nostrils the breath of
lives', of divers lives. Though our naturall life were no life, but
rather a continuall dying, yet we have two lives besides that, an
eternall life reserved for heaven, but yet a heavenly life too, a spirituall life, even in this world; And as God doth thus inflict two deaths,
and infuse two lives, so doth he also passe two Judgements upon
man, or rather repeats the same Judgement twice. For, that which
Christ shall say to thy soule then at the last Judgement, 'Enter into
thy Master's joy', Hee sayes to thy conscience now, 'Enter into thy
Master's joy'. The everlastingnesse of the joy is the blessednesse of
the next life, but the entring, the inchoation is afforded here. For
that which Christ shall say then to us, Venite benedicti, 'Come ye
blessed', are words intended to persons that are comming, that are
upon the way, though not at home; Here in this world he bids us
'Come', there in the next, he shall bid us 'Welcome'. The Angels
of heaven have joy in thy conversion, and canst thou bee without
that joy in thy selfe? If thou desire revenge upon thine enemies, as
they are God's enemies, That God would bee pleased to remove,
and root out all such as oppose him, that Affection appertaines
to Glory; Let that alone till thou come to the Hemisphear of
Glory; There joyne with these Martyrs under the Altar, Usquequo
Domine, 'How long, O Lord', dost thou deferre judgement? And
thou shalt have thine answere there for that. Whilst thou art here,
here joyne with David and the other Saints of God, in that holy
increpation of a dangerous sadnesse, 'Why art thou cast downe
O my soule? Why art thou disquieted in mee?' That soule that is

dissected and anatomized to God, in a sincere confession, washed in the teares of true contrition, embalmed in the blood of reconcilia-tion, the blood of Christ Jesus, can assigne no reason, can give no just answer to that Interrogatory, 'Why art thou cast downe O my soule? Why art thou disquieted in me?'

No man is so little as that he can be lost under these wings, no man so great, as that they cannot reach to him; Semper ille major est, quantumcumque creverimus, To what temporall, to what spirituall greatnesse soever wee grow, still pray wee him to shadow us under his Wings; for the poore need those wings against oppression, and the rich against envy.

The Holy Ghost, who is a Dove, shadowed the whole world under his wings; Incubabat aquis, He hovered over the waters, he sate upon the waters, and he hatched all that was produced, and all that was produced so, was good. Be thou a Mother where the Holy Ghost would be a Father; Conceive by him; and be content that he produce joy in thy heart here. First thinke, that as a man must have some land, or els he cannot be in wardship, so a man must have some of the love of God, or els he could not fall under God's correction; God would not give him his physick, God would not study his cure, if he cared not for him. And then thinke also, that if God afford thee the shadow of his wings, that is, Consolation, respiration, refreshing, though not a present, and plenary deliverance, in thy afflictions, not to thanke God, is a murmuring, and not to rejoyce in Gods wayes, is an unthankfulnesse.

Howling is the noyse of hell, singing the voyce of heaven; Sad-nesse the damp of Hell, Rejoycing the serenity of Heaven. And he that hath not this joy here, lacks one of the best pieces of his evidence for the joyes of heaven; and hath neglected or refused that Earnest, by which God uses to binde his bargaine, that true joy in this world shall flow into the joy of Heaven, as a River flowes into the Sea. This joy shall not be put out in death, and a new joy kindled in me in Heaven, but as my soule, as soone as it is out of my body, is in Heaven, and does not stay for the possession of Heaven, nor for the fruition of the sight of God, till it be ascended through ayre, and fire, and Moone, and Sun, and Planets, and Firmament, to that place which we conceive to be Heaven, but without the thousandth part of a minute's stop, as soone as it issues, is in a glorious light, which is Heaven, (for all the way to Heaven is Heaven; And as those Angels, which came from Heaven hither, bring Heaven with them, and are in Heaven here, So that soule that goes to Heaven, meets Heaven here; and as those Angels doe not devest Heaven by comming, so these soules invest Heaven, in their going.)

As my soule shall not goe towards Heaven, but goe by Heaven to Heaven, to the Heaven of Heavens, So the true joy of a good soule in this world is the very joy of Heaven; and we goe thither, not that being without joy, we might have joy infused into us, but that as Christ sayes, 'Our joy might be full', perfected, sealed with an ever-lastingnesse; for, as he promises, that 'no man shall take our joy' from us, so neither shall Death it selfe take it away, nor so much as interrupt it, or discontinue it. But as in the face of Death, when he layes hold upon me, and in the face of the Devill, when he attempts me, I shall see the face of God (for, every thing shall be a glasse, to reflect God upon me), so in the agonies of Death, in the anguish of that dissolution, in the sorrowes of that valediction, in the irreversi-blenesse of that transmigration, I shall have a joy, which shall no more evaporate, than my soule shall evaporate, A joy, that shall passe up, and put on a more glorious garment above, and be joy super-invested in glory. Amen.

Rest in hardship
Stephen Langton

Stephen Langton (1150–1228) was Archbishop of Canterbury, and to him is attributed the Sequence sung on Whitsun, the first half of which appears here.

Veni Sancte spiritus
et emitte coelitus
lucis tuae radium.

Veni pater pauperum;
veni dator munerum;
veni lumen cordium.

Consolator optime,
dulcis hospes animae,
dulce refrigerium.

In labore requies,
in aestu temperies,
in fletu solatium.

O lux beatissima,
reple cordis intima
tuorum fidelium.

Come, Holy Spirit, and send out a ray of your heavenly light. Come, father of the poor; come, giver of gifts; come, light of our hearts. The best of comforters, sweet guest of our soul, sweet freshness, rest in hardship, coolness in summer heat, relief in pain. O most blessed light, fill the innermost hearts of your faithful.

Many are His uses
Lancelot Andrewes

Lancelot Andrewes (1555–1626) was learned and holy and Bishop of Winchester. He is buried at Southwark Cathedral near to the house where he lived by the Thames. This first part of a sermon for Whitsun, preached before King James I at Windsor Castle in 1611, advises us not to treat the Holy Spirit merely as a convenient emergency service.

John 16:7. Yet I tell you the truth; it is expedient for you that I go away: for if I go not away, the Comforter will not come unto you; but if I depart, I will send Him unto you.

Sed Ego veritatem dico vobis; expedit vobis, ut Ego vadam: si enim non abiero, Paracletus non veniet ad vos; si autem abiero, mittam Eum ad vos.

If He go not, the Holy Ghost will not come. But, if Christ go, will He come? Shall we not be left to the wide world without both? Will the Comforter come? He will; for Christ will not fail but send Him. If He take His body from our eyes, He will send His Spirit into our hearts. But sent He shall be; here is *mittam Eum*, and so He did. Christ sent Him, and He came; and in memory of this *veniet et mittam*, hold we this day.

He did, to them; but will He also to us? He will. And shall we see 'fiery tongues?' That is not Christ's promise, to send 'fiery tongues'; but Illum, 'Him', 'the Comforter'. And comfort it is we seek. It is not the 'tongues,' or 'fire', we care for, or will do us good.

We conceive, I trust, after two manners He came as this day:

1. One visible, 'in tongues of fire that sat upon their heads';
2. The other invisible, by inward graces whereby He possessed their hearts.

The former was but for ceremony at first; the other is it, the real matter, Illum, 'Him'. And Him this day as well as that, this day and ever, He will not fail to send. Always we are to think His promise and His prayer were not for these only, but for all that should believe on Him, by their word, to the world's end.

Now this last point – these two, 1. mittam, 2. Illum – we are specially to look to. Christ is gone, once for all. We have no hold now but of this promise, 'I will send Him.' That we take heed we forego not Him, and lose our part in the promise too. A great part of the world is sure in this case: Christ is gone, and the Comforter is not sent. Not this; for I speak not of the world's comfort, the rich man's, qui habebat hic consolationem, 'who had his comfort here', in good fare and bravery, and all manner delights of the flesh – flesh-comforts; but this here is Paracletus Qui est Spiritus.

And because all religions promise a spiritual comfort, it is said further, Paracletus Qui est Spiritus veritatis; no spirit of error, but 'the Spirit of Truth'. And because all Christians, though counterfeit, claim an interest in Spiritus veritatis, yet further it is added, Paracletus qui est Spiritus Sanctus. He is no unclean Spirit, but one sanctifying, and leading us into an holy and clean life. This is the true Comforter, and none other, that Christ promiseth to send.

Christ will send Him. But, that we mistake Him not, not unless we call for Him, and be ready to entertain Him, for cletus is in Paracletus. Of which let me tell you these three things; it is the chief word of the text, and chief thing of the Feast. It is translated 'Comforter': that translation is, but ad homines, for their turn to whom He speaks; for as their case was, they needed that office of His most. But the true force of the word paracletus is advocatus – not the noun but the participle – 'one called to', sent for, invited to come, upon what occasion, or for what end soever it be. For what end soever it be, the person sent for is paracletus properly, pro ea vice; for that time and turn, advocatus.

But because 'the spirit of the world' ruleth in this world, the worldly affairs come thickest, our affections in that kind so many and oft, it is come to pass that the lawyer hath carried away the name of advocatus from the rest, and they grown to be the paracleti of this world, called for even from the Prince to the Peasant, and consulted with, none so often. The Physician, he hath his time and turn of advocation, to be a paracletus too, but nothing so oft: as for Barnabas, which is interpreted 'the son of consolation', never till both 'Zenas the Lawyer', and 'Luke the Physician' have given us over; never called for, but when it is too late.

But first, from mittam Paracletum, this we have. Mittam, Christ 'will send'; but Paracletum, if you send for Him. Veniet, 'come He will', but not come, unless called; nor sent, but sent for. If we call Him, veniet, 'He will come'; if we send for Him, He will send Him. That is our duty, but what is our practice? We miss in this first, we call not for Him. We find no time for Him, He is fain to call for us, to ring a bell for us, to send about to get us, and then are we advocati, not He. When we send for Him, He is Paracletus; when He for us, then we are, and not He: – if we be that, if we be advocati and not rather avocati, every trifling occasion being enough to call us away. Thus we stumble at the very threshold; and do we yet marvel if Christ send Him not, nor He come?

Men are sent for for some end; and divers are the ends, thereafter as our need is. We send not for them only when we are in heaviness, to comfort us, but when we are in doubt, to resolve us; which is the second signification, and so Paracletus is turned 'advocate', or 'counsellor'. And the Holy Ghost looketh to be sent for for both – for counsel, as well as for consolation. For both; He is good for both. Yea, many are His uses; and therefore He thinketh much to be sent for but for one, as if He were good for nothing else. If we be in doubt, He is able to resolve us; if perplexed, to advise and to guide; if we know not how, to frame our petition for us; if we know not, to teach; if we forget, to remember us; and not only one use, as we fancy, if we be out of heart, to comfort us.

And because His uses be many, His types are so. 'Water' sometimes, sometimes 'fire'. One while 'wind', one while 'ointment'; and according to our several wants we send to Him: for fire, to warm; for wind, to cool; for water, to cleanse us; for oil, to supply us. And as His types, so His names: 'the Spirit of truth', 'the Spirit of counsel', the 'Spirit of holiness', 'the Spirit of comfort'. And according to His several faculties, we to invocate, or call for, Him by that name that is most for our use or present occasion. For all these, He looks we should send for Him.

Our error is, as if He were only for one use or office – for comfort alone: so, in all others we let Him alone, and if never in heaviness, never look after Him, or care once to hear of Him. But He is for advice, and direction also. No less Paracletus, 'a counsellor', than Paracletus, 'a comforter'; He is not sent by Christ to comfort only. Ye may see by the very next words: the first thing He doth when He cometh is, He shall 'reprove', which is far from comforting. But sent He is, as well to mediate with us for God, as with God for us. God's

Paracletus, 'His Solicitor', to call on us for our duty; as our Paracletus, or 'Comforter', to minister us comfort in time of need.

Our manner is, we love to be left to ourselves, in our consultations to advise with flesh and blood, thence to take our direction, all our life; and when we must part, then send for Him for a little comfort, and there is all the use we have of Him. But he that will have comfort from Him, must also take counsel of Him; have use of Him as well against error and sinful life, as against heaviness of mind. If not, here is your doom: where you have had your counsel, there seek your comfort; he that hath been your counsellor all the time of your life, let him be your comforter at the hour of your death. And good reason: He will not be Paracletus at halves, to stand by at all else, and only to be sent for in our infirmity.

Joy and peace
Gregory XIII

Pope Gregory XIII (1502–85) has had the composition of this prayer attributed to him.

Gaudium cum pace, emendationem vitae, spatium verae poenitentiae, gratiam et consolationem Sancti Spiritus, perseverantiam in bonis operibus, tribuat nobis omnipotens et misericors Dominus. Amen.

May the almighty and merciful Lord grant us joy and peace, amendment of life, time for true repentance, the grace and consolation of the Holy Spirit and perseverance in good works. Amen.

God's gift of God
H.A. Williams

Harry Williams (born 1919), a fellow of Trinity College, Cambridge, from 1951 to 1959, impressed a generation of undergaduates with his re-examination of what it means to be a Christian. For himself, he laid aside all pretence, and in 1969, aged 50, he resigned his fellowship and joined the Community of the Resurrection at Mirfield, Yorkshire. The passage here comes from his book The Joy of God *(1979).*

It belongs to the gods that are for sale to offer instant and more or less continuous pleasure, whether it be the pleasure of excitement or of tranquillization. And not only those pleasures either, but goodies like success, happiness, freedom from distress, and in general health and wealth. We are reminded of Mrs Whittaker (who, unlike her sister, married well) in Dorothy Parker's short story: 'Mrs Whittaker's attitude of kindly tolerance was not confined to her less fortunate relatives. It extended to friends of her youth, working people, the arts, politics, the United States in general and God, who had always supplied her with the best of service. She could have given Him an excellent reference at any time.'

But when the god fails to deliver the goods, be it excitement, tranquillization, well-being or whatever, he is dropped – thrown away like a broken gadget. And even when he does keep what is considered his side of the bargain, he leaves hunger in the heart (all the worse for being smothered) as all things of this earth alone are bound to do. Religion as a species of insurance, sedation or joy-popping cannot fail to betray its devotees.

It is bracing to turn from these gods for sale (which are no gods) to the testimony of a man of profound religious insight and devotion, a high authority on Christian mysticism, Friedrich von Hügel, who wrote towards the end of his long life: 'Religion has never made me happy; it's no use shutting your eyes to the fact that the deeper you go, the more alone you will find yourself. . . . Religion has never made me comfy. I have been in the desert ten years. All deepened life is deepened suffering, deepened dreariness, deeper joy. Suffering and joy. The final note of religion is joy.'

God is not for sale. He cannot be bought. In spite of appearances to the contrary, the churches, when true to themselves, know that they are not stalls at Vanity Fair and that all they can do is

180

encourage people to discover the true God for themselves. People can do this because, as St Paul is reported to have said at Athens: 'God is not far from each one of us, for in Him we live and move and have our being.' If ultimately only God can satisfy our infinite longing, only He fill the hole in our heart, it might look as if we had to set out on a desperate search for Him. And because the words of earth can only most indirectly and obliquely indicate the realities of heaven, there is a sense in which we do indeed have to search for God, to seek if we are to find, to knock if it is to be opened to us. But it is an odd sort of searching, for it ends with the discovery that God is and has been with us all the time, that He is not far off, but nearer to us than the air we breathe, and that, like the air, His presence with us is not something we have earned, but is a free gift to all. Because we can speak of God only obliquely, in our talk about Him we shall get tied up in all sorts of inconsistent spatial metaphors. That doesn't matter. What godly men try to tell us makes sense in spite of the apparent contradictions.

We discover God as our environment. In the homely imagery of the psalmist, He is about our path and about our bed and familiar with all our ways. It is in Him, to quote St Paul again, that we live and move and have our being. But if God is around us He is also within us. And if He is within us it is not as an alien, not as Another, but as our truest selves. A human individual with a powerful personality may be said to invade us as an alien, destroying our autonomy and forcing us into his own mould so that we lose our own identity and become mere copies of his. The same thing happens on the rare occasions when sexual passion reaches a pitch of almost demonic proportions as when Catherine Earnshaw says to her old nurse: 'Nellie, I am Heathcliff.'

But unlike another human being, God is our creator, and by dwelling within us He makes us our own true selves and establishes our personal identity. He negates Himself in us in order to find Himself in us. That is to say, He limits Himself so that, instead of overwhelming us, He gradually and gently calls forth into being the tender, vulnerable fragility of our true selfhood, the fragility which when made perfect is also stronger than steel. And in this continuous creative work within us, which is His presence, it is Himself which He discovers in us. 'God begins to live in me,' says Thomas Merton, 'not only as my creator but as my other and true self' – other and true because I spend much of my time fabricating a false self instead of allowing God to create me.

When we consider God's relationship to the self we are often misled by concentrating too exclusively on one particular spatial metaphor. God is above us, we say. Well, from one point of view, of course He is above us, infinitely so. He is our creator and there is an infinite difference between God and what He creates. But God's relationship to us is not an outside relationship in which He is in one place and we in another. As our creator God is the ground of our being, the fount from which we continually flow. The self I am is constituted by its relationship to God as its deepest centre. If God gives us the gift of infinite difference from Himself, He also gives us the gift of identity with Himself, a truth summarized by St Paul in his statement: 'I live; yet not I, but Christ liveth in me.' 'God utters me like a word containing a partial thought of Himself ... If I am true to the concept God utters in me, if I am true to the thought of Him I was meant to embody, I shall be full of His actuality and find Him everywhere in myself.' It is a truth which can bear emphasizing as it comes strangely to many Christians. Let us therefore listen to the 17th-century Catholic mystic – he was a Pole – Angelus Silesius:

> Stop, where dost thou run?
> God's heaven is in thee.
> If thou seekest it elsewhere
> Never shalt thou see!
> In good time we shall see
> God and His light you say!
> Fool, never shall you see
> What you don't see today.

Or we could listen to the down-to-earth 18th-century Jesuit Jean Pierre de Caussade, who wrote: 'Truly, said Jacob, God is in this place and I knew it not. You seek God and He is everywhere; everything proclaims Him, everything gives Him to you. He walks by your side, is around you and within you: there He lives, and yet you seek Him. You seek your own idea of God while all the time you possess Him substantially [i.e. in fullest possible reality].'

If God so made us that only He Himself can ultimately satisfy us, He does not withhold that gift of Himself. It is ours already, but, being too blind to recognize it, we have to discover it, not in religious theory, but in the warmth and sweetness and dryness and terror of actual living.

Walking with God

Everything in the ark
Hugh of St Victor

Hugh of St Victor (1096–1141) got his surname from the monastery of St Victor in Paris, renowned for piety and learning, which he entered in 1116. He spent the rest of his life there, gaining an unrivalled familiarity with the Fathers of the Church, becoming a popular lecturer, and resisting the damaging reductivism of Peter Abelard's philosophy. He was a mystic too, and with this approach to God wrote De Arca Noe, *'On Noah's Ark'. The short extract here shows a deliberate equation of Noah's ark with the ark of the covenant, both of which the heart resembles as the dwelling place of God.*

Now, therefore, enter your own inmost heart, and make a dwelling-place for God. Make Him a temple, make Him a house, make Him a pavilion. Make Him an ark of the covenant, make Him an ark of the flood; no matter what you call it, it is all one house of God. In the temple let the creature adore the Creator, in the house let the son revere the Father, in the pavilion let the knight adore the King. Under the covenant, let the disciple listen to the Teacher. In the flood, let him that is shipwrecked beseech Him who guides the helm.

God is become everything to you, and God has made everything for you. He has made the dwelling, and is become your refuge. This one is all, and this all is one. It is the house of God, it is the city of the King, it is the body of Christ, it is the bride of the Lamb. It is the heaven, it is the sun, it is the moon, it is the morning star, the day-break and the evening. It is the trumpet, it is the mountain, and the desert, and the promised land. It is the ship, it is the way across the sea. It is the net, the vine, the field. It is the ark, the barn, the stable, and the manger. It is the beast of burden, and it is the horse. It is the storehouse, the court, the wedding-chamber, the tower, the camp, the battle-front. It is the people, and the kingdom, and the priesthood. It is the flock and the shepherd, the sheep and the pastures. It is paradise, it is the garden, it is the palm, the rose, the lily. It is the fountain and the river; it is the door, it is the dove, it is the raiment, it is the pearl, it is the crown, it is the sceptre, and it is the throne. It is the table and the bread, it is the spouse, the mother, the daughter and the sister.

And, to sum it all up, it was for this, with a view to this, on account of this, that the whole of Scripture was made. For this, the Word was made flesh, God was made humble, man was made sublime.

If you have this, then you have everything. If you have everything, you have nothing more to look for, and your heart is at rest.

A turn in the gallery
John Spencer

John Spencer in writing of conversation with God takes the fact that in the 17th century big houses had a gallery upstairs along one side, perhaps with family portraits in, but anyway designed for a walk at leisure in the afternoon if the weather outdoors was not inviting.

The true Love of God will cause familiarity with God

Where there is Love free from jealousie betwixt Man and Wife, they are, as it were, incorporated; they think themselves never better than when they are in one another's company, talking and discoursing together, laying open each other's griefs, and making one another partaker of each other's comforts. So, we must have such interest in God, if we love him, we must in an humble distanced manner be familiar with him. Let never a day pass over our heads wherein we have not fetched a walk or two in the gallery of our hearts with him, and there laid open our selves before him, both concerning our miseries and our Sins, saying after this or the like manner; Thou seest, O Lord, what sorrowes I endure within or without, I beseech thee, give me grace, so to carry my self, as that thou mayest have the glory of thy own work; And thou knowest, O my God, that I have this infirmity, or that weaknesse; and that were it not for thee, I should falle into fearfull breaches of thy Law; but, Lord, help me against this or that sin, as against Pride, deceit, vain-glory, and the like, that I may be in a more settled and constant course honour thee, my God, to whom I am so infinitely bound.

Religion of love
John Wesley

John Wesley (1703–91) worked with breathtaking energy to preach and bring people to a knowledge of God. Though he remained a clergyman in the Church of England, his followers formed the Methodist connexion. All along he was concerned with the heart of Christianity, the love of God. The passage here comes from An Earnest Appeal to Men of Reason and Religion *(1743).*

I once saw one, who, from a plentiful fortune, was reduced to the lowest extremity. He was lying on a sick bed, in violent pain, without even convenient food, or one friend to comfort him. So that when his merciful landlord, to complete all, sent one to take his bed from under him, I was not surprised at his attempt to put an end to so miserable a life. Now, when I saw that poor man weltering in his blood, could I be angry at him? Surely, no. No more can I at you. I can no more hate than I can envy you. I can only lift up my heart to God for you, (as I did then for him) and, with silent tears; beseech the Father of Mercies, that he would look on you in your blood, and say unto you, 'Live'.

'Sir,' said that unhappy man, at my first interview with him, 'I scorn to deceive you or any man. You must not tell me of your Bible, for I do not believe one word of it. I know there is a God and believe he is all in all, the Anima mundi, the Totam mens agitans molem, et magno se corpore miscens. But farther than this I believe not. All is dark; my thought is lost.' 'But I hear,' added he, 'you preach to a great number of people every night and morning. Pray, what would you do with them? Whither would you lead them? What religion do you preach? What is it good for?'

I replied, 'I do preach to as many as desire to hear, every night and morning. You ask, what I would do with them: I would make them virtuous and happy, easy in themselves, and useful to others. Whither would I lead them? To heaven; to God the Judge, the lover of all, and to Jesus the Mediator of the new covenant. What religion do I preach? The religion of love; the law of kindness brought to light by the gospel. What is this good for? To make all who receive it enjoy God and themselves: To make them like God; lovers of all; contented in their lives; and crying out at their death, in calm assurance; "O grave, where is thy victory! Thanks be unto God, who giveth me the victory, through my Lord Jesus Christ." '

Strengthening
Philip Doddridge

Philip Doddridge (1702–51) was the 20th child of a Bohemian Lutheran preacher's daughter who had married a prosperous English Nonconformist merchant. Of the children only one other, his sister Elizabeth, survived to maturity.

Doddridge was ordained presbyter by Presbyterian ministers in 1730. He undertook ministry in Northampton, where a mob attacked his house in 1736. In that year he received the degree of Doctor of Divinity from Aberdeen, and undertook the organization of an academy for dissenters, enjoining the students to take full notes of his well-constructed lectures in shorthand.

It was Doddridge's aim to bring unity to the divided ranks of English Nonconformity. He was himself essentially a Calvinist, but he entertained the strange belief that the human soul of Jesus Christ pre-existed his birth in Bethlehem. And it has to be admitted that most of his pupils leant towards Arianism, the belief that the person of Jesus Christ is not uncreated God equal with the father.

Doddridge's life, shortened by consumptive weakness, was almost overwhelmed by his undertakings in teaching, corresponding and writing. He tried

187

natural baths as a cure, and the Bishop of Worcester offered the use of his car-
riage; he went to Portugal for his health and the Countess of Huntingdon (the
Calvinist ally of Wesley) helped pay. He died in Lisbon, just before the publi-
cation of the sixth and final volume of his Family Expositor. *It is clearly a*
work intended for well-to-do Nonconformists, like his own father, for it is
printed in type that is large and elegant (a favourite word of Doddridge's) on
paper in a quarto format with wide margins, intended to be bound up in the calf
of the purchaser's choice and read out by the paterfamilias day by day.

Part of Doddridge's success was that he knew his audience, and if he makes
St Paul sound like a wordy Georgian preacher in a horsehair wig, well that was
the fashionable style. The Expositor has a three-layered structure. In the mar-
gin is the text of the New Testament book under consideration; in the main body
of the page is a paraphrase, descanting on the biblical wording; following this is
an Improvement, that is, a practical consideration for the reader – or listen-
ers – to take to heart. The comfort that he considers here is partly strengthening
and partly consolation.

2. Thessalonians, 2:16

And may our Lord Jesus Christ, and GOD even our Father, who
hath loved us in so surprising a Manner, and given us by his Gospel
such a Fund of everlasting Consolation, and such good Hope thro'
his overflowing Grace, when, without it, we could not have had any
Glimmering of Hope, or Prospect of Comfort for ever – May he, I
say, by the rich Communication of his Love and Mercy, comfort
your Hearts, and may he strengthen and confirm you, making you
ready for every good Word and Work, that his Name may be glorified, and your present Satisfaction and future Reward may abound.
As for what remains, I shall not enlarge, but must beseech you,
Brethren that ye would pray for us, that the Word of the Lord may
run a free and unobstructed Course every where, and be greatly
glorified, as through his Grace it is among you.

IMPROVEMENT
Blessed be GOD, who in this View hath called us to obtain Salvation
and Glory by Jesus Christ, even GOD our Father who hath loved us.

From him do these everlasting Consolations flow. It is by his blessed and gracious Operation, we are strengthened and established in every good Word and Work. His Fidelity stands engaged to do it, if we humbly commit ourselves to him. The prayers of the Apostles, dictated no doubt from above, concur with the Promises to encourage our Hopes that he will direct our Hearts into the Love of GOD and the Patience of Jesus Christ. On the Exercise of that Love and that Patience doth the Happiness of our Life chiefly depend. Too ready are our weak Hearts to wander from it, and to faint under the Difficulties that lie in our Way. Let us call on him to preserve and maintain the Graces he hath implanted, that they may be exerted with growing Vigour and Constancy even unto the End.

Never mind the weather
Mark Allen and Ruth Burrows

Mark Allen (born 1950), a British diplomat, entered into an exchange of letters on prayer with Ruth Burrows (born 1924), a Carmelite nun who has written a series of acclaimed books on the spiritual life. Here he wonders what consolation we can expect once we are committed to persevere in prayer that is an exercise of faith in God.

Very dear Ruth,

Your last letter reached me in these remote hills, wild now with cloud and rain. I don't really feel like walking and there's a cold breeze which seems to be coming out of Russia. So it has been good to have your letter to reflect on by a June fireside.

You said something very important about consolations and I hope you will develop that. Here I am going to try to set out what I find are the difficult edges. It may give you something against which to draw out your thoughts.

'Gazing into the face of Christ, we know ...' You wrote this in answer to questions I was asking about 'communications'. Your answers helped me to see that faith asks us not to dwell on any impression or experience and take it as being of the Father. What occurs to us is not God. We have to let these things go. What we have is the Word, the enduring gift which the Father has sent. The Word, however, itself tells only of the Father as beyond and yet present, having spoken and yet resounding.

We have to be able to admit, don't we, that we can have heard the Word? How? Here what you say about the heart is convincing. In our living, we realize that the Word is at work in us, is being heard and even listened to in us, and if not by me, then certainly by another. And this is apparent to us because, as the years pass, we know new depths, we see new things in once familiar sights. We can affirm that we are touched by the Word and also that we are indirectly deepened by experience. This for me is why silent, unoccupied prayer is a way that must be walked: it is placing our capacity to be touched and to experience at the disposal intentionally of God. And the heart of this is that because we usually experience nothing in prayer, we are brought starkly before that imperative of faith – not to settle down, but to look ahead without any sensible hope at the time of being able to see anything. This unoccupied prayer leaves the self open and exposed not only to the secret work of God, but also to some experience of itself. And this experience is purifying. Prayer, as time goes by, cannot but leave us a little humbler, a little more persuaded that we have to act to change, have to surrender to that call of love, have to trust to faith: all that you write about choice. In this, I see what is meant by the, at first baffling, idea that prayer is the best thing, the most important thing we can do.

'Gaze into the face of Christ . . .' I could never say that I have done that. My literal mind can't make sense of it. And my heart? I can say that I can only understand what takes place in my life, looking back over it and holding on to the objective reality of the Word, as being an exposure to the action, yes, of a person. That person, in faith, I take to be Christ: ever secretly present, ever consistent and consonant with his unceasing revelation of himself in the Word.

That this action in the world is a person, I saw particularly through the optic of that astonishing book *God For Us* by your late friend, Catherine Mowry LaCugna. She examines the idea that personhood in Jesus, and therefore also in us, is 'ecstasis of nature' – the giving out of itself, the giving away of the self. Our experience of others and ourselves is of a personhood which reveals and utters our flawed natures; whereas the person of Christ, the Word, resonates the perfection of the Father's will which is Love. In this living for his Father's will, Jesus gives away that inexhaustible goodness. His action of living for others makes his life an ecstasis of his nature which is received from the Father and is absolute goodness. LaCugna quotes from St Augustine, 'Because God is good, we exist.' We are called to personhood: to be, to give away, to pass on what we are given, in sacrifice of love.

The heart, empowered by faith, can sense but cannot comprehend that goodness. The passing experience of life reveals it as better yet than we could have believed before, and so on. But if this is consolation, the mystery of the sacrifice of the cross tells also of a goodness and love which cannot rest, but must go on, beyond what was conceivable before. The realization that in this there is truly a person at work dawns with the sense that none of this is our doing. All is done for us and through the sacramental life of the Church as we receive from others: persons enacting the goodness we receive through Christ, the Person who in the Spirit is at work in the goodness of people. Jesus himself tells us the truth about goodness, 'Why do you call me good? No one is good but God alone' (Mark 10:18).

So the idea that there is a Person active in sustaining each of our lives, which might at first appear to be consoling – a comfortable arrangement of the dismaying muddle of life – is not so at all. This is a Person of a different order whom we may understand only by surrendering to a call that we ourselves become persons in a new sense from what we ordinarily understand. On the staircase of this journey, my banister, like a piece of rock, has one word running through it: Hope. Hope does help. There's no doubt about it. Can you draw out a distinction between hope and consolation?

How do these thoughts track what was in your mind when you wrote of 'gazing into the face of Christ'?

With much love ,

Mark

Dearest Mark,

Thank you for your letter. I sympathize with you having had to sit by a fire in so-called flaming June with that glorious, rolling countryside outside your windows, curtained with cloud and rain. 'It's an ill wind . . .', however, and it gave you opportunity for reflection. Your normal lifestyle is very pressured. I myself have time for reflection as I go about my household jobs, but not so much time for getting down to writing letters. However, here goes.

'Gazing into the face of Christ' means, I believe, the same as listening to the Word. It's an echo of Paul's 'light of the knowledge of the glory of God in the face of Christ' (2 Corinthians 4:6). As I understand it – and I am sure I have said it all before – it's, so to speak, a double process: we do what we can to learn about Christ Jesus, that is, with our ordinary faculties, to learn what we can of him and his vision of God and created reality, trying at the same time to conform our minds and our actions to him. This loving effort opens us to the hidden action of God within and through this hidden action we are gradually transformed into his likeness. We gaze 'outwardly' with our normal faculties and, through divine gift, are shown 'inwardly.' I understand it as sacramental in nature.

We hear the Word, really choose to listen to it which means affirming it and trying to live by it, and then its content, the Word, is received. I think most of Chapter 6 of the gospel of John is precisely about this sacrament of the Word. 'It was not Moses who gave you the bread from heaven; it is my Father who gives you the bread from heaven, the true bread; for the bread of God is the bread which comes down from heaven and gives life to the world' (John 6:32–3). In the scriptural sense, as well you know, 'Word' embraces works as well as words: everything audible, visual and tangible and supremely, Jesus himself. With you, I am convinced that what we call 'unoccupied prayer' is a great act of faith that affirms implicitly that God communicates lovingly with us, at our centre, purifying and transforming us. What we have to insist on over and over again is that this divine communication, because divine, is not available to our ordinary faculties and is, therefore, hidden. Hence the sharpness of the test of faith.

Mark, I think we should leave the subject of consolations, as I feel that, by discussing it further we are giving it a prominence it does not have. I think I have exhausted my thought on it. What's more, I feel a lot of reflection and analysis of it can make us self-conscious of our praying self, whereas real prayer is 'off' self, uninterested in how it is going, what is experienced and so forth. We go on praying whatever the weather outside or in. It's as simple as that. Of course, we all like lovely sunshine and find life easier when there is plenty of it. But we in this country surely know how to adapt ourselves to weather and not to bank on a lovely day for this, that or the other. Surely we know how to get on with life in spite of the weather? And, after all, hasn't our 'weather' something to do with the formation of our natural character, our enterprise and capacity to soldier on doggedly? Inclement weather has advantages! I feel we should aim at real indifference to weather conditions: getting on with living for God and others without much reflection on how we are feeling spiritually.

Once again I hold up Thérèse of Lisieux, truly the saint of ordinary folk like ourselves. 'Lord, you give me joy in all You do.' She was suffering atrociously in mind and body when she penned those words. This was faith, hope and love against all sensible feeling and this is what we try for. It's the joy Jesus wants to share with us, his joy which no one and nothing can ever deprive us of. 'Hitherto you have asked nothing in my name; ask and you will receive that your joy may be full' (John 16:24). To my mind, this has nothing to do with sensible joy though it may at times be accompanied by it. It is the joy, the solid content, the hope of absolute fulfilment based solely on Reality, the Reality of Abba as revealed by Jesus. And if we do want to look for real consolation, here it is. Sense may know little of it but the inmost heart knows and therefore can stand undaunted in every kind of spiritual weather and can humbly hope, relying on the 'promise of the Father' that, should great suffering come, it will still cry out in trust: 'Abba, my Father.' I think that Paul especially is the proclaimer of hope. 'We walk by faith and not by sight' (2 Corinthians 5:7) and yet have certain, unshakeable hope through the gift of the Spirit poured into our hearts.

Most eloquent for me are two short passages, the first from the Epistle to the Romans (1:1): 'Since we are justified by faith, we have peace with God through our Lord Jesus Christ. Through him we have obtained access to this grace in which we stand, and we rejoice in our hope of sharing the glory of God. More than that, we rejoice in our sufferings, knowing that suffering produces endurance, and endurance produces character, and character produces hope, and hope does not disappoint us, because God's love has been poured into our hearts through the Holy Spirit which has been given to us.'

Secondly, from the Second Epistle to the Corinthians (1:3), there is this: 'Blessed be the God and Father of our Lord Jesus Christ, the Father of mercies and God of all comfort, who comforts us in all our affliction, so that we may be able to comfort those who are in any affliction, with the comfort with which we ourselves are comforted by God. For as we share abundantly in Christ's sufferings, so through Christ we share abundantly in comfort too.'

It is by faith and hope that we surrender ourselves to the Mystery of God who is Love absolute and this surrender is love. True love is ecstatic, outside self, a letting go of self and abdicating to Another. Herein lies personhood, a faint echo we surmise, of what we mean by 'person' when speaking of the Trinity. But, of course, we have Jesus our brother to show us and enable us to be truly human, truly person and just what that is, we cannot know in this life. We shall know when, for each of us, God is revealed, seen as God really is and in that vision, we become like Him and know our own reality which is reality only in Him. I believe that the transforming revelation

194

begins in this life, in darkness and concealment. We must wait in
hope for the revelation of our divine 'sonship'.

I'm not confident, dear Mark, that I have entered into your
thought expressed in this letter before me, but I have tried to do so
and offer you these reflections of mine as the best I can do.

With my love,

Ruth

Batter my heart
John Donne

*John Donne (1572–1631) in this sonnet almost challenges God to do him vio-
lence so that he can be made anew.*

Batter my heart, three person'd God; for, you
As yet but knocke, breathe, shine, and seeke to mend;
That I may rise, and stand, o'erthrow mee, and bend
Your force, to breake, blowe, burn and make me new.
I, like an usurpt towne, to another due,
Labour to admit you, but Oh, to no end,
Reason your viceroy in mee, mee should defend,
But is captiv'd, and proves weake or untrue.
Yet dearely I love you, and would be loved faine,
But am betroth'd unto your enemie:
Divorce mee, untie, or breake that knot againe,
Take mee to you, imprison mee, for I
Except you enthrall mee, never shall be free,
Nor ever chast, except you ravish mee.

Ebb and flow
Thomas à Kempis

*Thomas à Kempis (1380–1471) recognizes that God does not always seem
near, but insists that trials are a sign of comfort coming soon. This translation*

'set forth in rhythmic sentences' was published in 1889 with a preface by the scholar and preacher H.P. Liddon.

Is it so great
To smile and be devout when God's touch comes to you?
This is an hour beloved by all.
He rides with ease
Drawn in a chariot of God's grace
What wonder if he feel no weight,
Carried by Almighty God,
And guided by the best of guides?

We are delighted to be comforted by something;
Man finds it hard to doff the garment of himself.

Laurence the martyr and his priest o'er came the world,
Despising all that seemed delightful in the universe,
And for Christ's love even suffered
That Sixtus should be taken from him,
Sixtus the high priest of God, whom he loved so much.
Thus by his love for his Creator he overcame his love of man,
And for human consolation he chose what pleased his God.
And you, too, learn to leave some close and much-loved
    friend, to show your love of God;
Nor take it grievously when you are left by one you love,
Knowing that we must all at last be parted.

Great and long must be the conflict in a man
Before he learns fully to win the battle o'er himself,
And draw his whole affection unto God.
When a man rests upon himself
He lightly slips to human comfort,
But Christ's true lover and the careful follower of the good
Does not fall back on consolation,
Nor does he seek deluding sweetness such as this,

196

But asks that he may rather bear
Hard labour and stern practices for Christ.

Therefore when comfort of the spirit is given from God
    to you,
Take it: be thankful;
But know – it is a gift of God,
And not a merit of your own.
Be not puffed up;
Do not rejoice nor emptily presume,
But be the humbler for the gift,
More careful and more timid in your actions;
For the hour of consolation will go by and trial will follow in
    its wake.
When comfort goes,
Do not at once despair,
But with humility and patience wait for the coming of the
    heavenly One;
For God can give you greater comfort than before.

This is nothing new nor strange
To those who knows God's way;
For in the lives of saints and seers of old
Often has it been like this –
One comfort changing for another.
Therefore one said when grace was with him,
'I said in my abundance,
I shall never be moved';
But, when God's favour went,
He tells us what he felt; and says,
'Thou didst turn Thy face from me,
And I was troubled.'
Yet even so, far from despairing,
He presses on his prayer to God, and says,
'To Thee, O God, I will lift up my voice,

197

And to my God lift up my prayer.'
At last he brings the good back from his prayer,
And witnesses that he was heard, and says,
'God heard and pitied me,
He is become my Helper.'
(And how?)
'Turning my wailing into joy,
Surrounding me with gladness.'

If the great saints have found it thus,
We, weak and poor, must not despair,
If at one hour we burn,
And at another hour are cold;
Because the Spirit ebbs and flows
At the good pleasure of God's will,
And blessed Job has said,
'At early dawn Thou comest to him,
And on a sudden provest him.'

But what, then, can I hope for,
And in what thing should I trust?
Even in God's great pity alone,
And in the hope of favour from on high.
For though good men be near me, pious brothers, faithful
    friends,
Sweet songs or hymns,
All these please me but a little,
Taste but a little,
When I am left by God and find myself in my own poverty.
Then there is no better remedy
Than patience and self-sacrifice beneath the will of God.

Never did I meet with man so pious, so devout,
Who, now and then, had not some lessening of God's
    kindness,

Who did not feel God's favour, now and then, grow smaller.
None so holy, so high wrought, so full of light,
Who has not been tempted, in days gone by, or now.
For he deserves not to enjoy a lofty thought of God,
Who is not tried for God by sorrow.
Trial is wont to be the sign of comfort coming soon;
For to men proved by trial
Heaven and consolation is vouchsafed, –
'To him that overcometh I will give for food the tree of life';
And consolation from on high is sent
To make us brave to bear adversity.
Temptation follows
That man may not be proud for blessings he has had.
The devil does not sleep,
And flesh is not yet dead.
Haste therefore to prepare you for the fray;
For on your right hand and your left
Stand foes who never rest.

Salamanders
John Spencer

John Spencer brings a very 17th-century catalogue from the natural world to show how God's children are improved by hardships and thrive, as salamanders were said to do, amid the fire.

A Child of God bettered by Afflictions

Stars shine brightest in the darkest night;
Grapes come not to the proof, till they come to the Presse;
Spices smell sweetest when pownded;
Young trees root the faster for shaking;
Vines are the better for bleeding;
Gold looks the brighter for scowring;
Glow-worms glister best in the dark;

Juniper smells sweetest in the fire;
Pomander becomes most fragrant for chafing;
The Palm-Tree proves the better for pressing;
Camomile, the more you tread it, the more you spread it:
Such is the condition of God's children;
They are then most triumphant when most tempted;
Most glorious when most afflicted;
Most in the favour of God when least to Man's;
As their Conflicts so their Conquests;
As their Tribulations, so their Triumphs:
True Salamanders, that live best in the Furnace of
    Persecution;
So that heavy Afflictions are the best Benefactors to
    Heavenly affections;
And where Afflictions hang heaviest, corruptions hang
    loosest:
And Grace that is hid in nature, as sweet water in
    Rose-leaves is then most
fragrant when the fire of Affliction is put under to distill it out.

Care in all times
Lucy Herbert

Lady Lucy Herbert (1669–1744) was the fifth daughter of the Marquess of Powis and his wife Elizabeth. She left everything at the age of twenty-four to join the convent of the Augustinian Canonesses at Bruges. To the sometimes formal devotional life of her day she brings warmth in recommending a spiritual friendship with one's Guardian Angel.

Take one day of each month to honour your good Angel, as, for example, the second Sunday in the month. After having employed one quarter of an hour after Communion in thanksgiving for the said favour, reflect upon the great goodness of that God you possess within you, who, knowing your weakness and the danger you are exposed to, both for soul and body, and the difficulty you have to defend yourself against your enemies, has appointed you one of His Angels, who are the princes of His Heavenly Court, and has given him orders to assist and defend you, and never to leave you as long as your soul is in your body.

Return His Divine Majesty most humble thanks for so infinite a favour, and admire the value He puts on your soul and the love He has for it, since He thus employs an Angel for your service. Then with great respect and humility, address yourself to your Angel Guardian and keeper. Thank him for accepting the charge of you, and, since on his part he promises you four things and faithfully performs them, do you the like, and be as faithful in your performance as he is.

1. He promises you to be ever present and never to abandon you.
2. To cherish and love you as a child of God, bought with His Blood, and designed for the same glory he enjoys.
3. To guard both your body and your soul, and to procure what is best for both.
4. To continue his care of you in all times and places, till your soul is separated from your body.

On your part, promise him also four things and beg his assistance for the performance.

1. A great reverence and respect to him, and neither to think, say, or do anything deliberately that may offend or displease him.
2. A great love and tender devotion to him, loving him as your father and best of friends, and endeavouring to increase his glory and joy in Heaven by the holiness of your life upon earth.
3. A great confidence in his care and protection over you, and to have recourse to him, as a child to the arms of its mother, in all your pains and difficulties, invoking his help in all.
4. To persevere in these duties till your last breath.

This contract being made between your good Angel and you, beg our dear Lord, whom you have received, to bestow His benediction upon it. Then retire in company of your good Angel, and from time to time entertain yourself with him the rest of the day. Sometimes thanking him for all the good turns he has done you from the day of your birth (which was the day he first began to take care of you) till this present moment, reflecting on the chief, and, next to God, attributing them to him.

Sometimes asking his pardon for having passed so many years of your life without thinking of him, or at least very little. And for having so often contristated him by your imperfections, and so seldom made your recourse to him in your necessities, or thanked him for his benefits.

At other times open your heart to him, declare to him your necessities, and beg him to solicit God in your behalf. Desire him to give you light in your doubts, help in your dangers, comfort in your afflictions, and victory over your enemies, with his particular assistance at the hour of your death.

Moreover, during the day address yourself to him by short aspirations, and if time will permit you, perform some devotion in his honour, as his Office, or litanies, or some colloquies.

Angels descending
Henry Vaughan

Henry Vaughan (1622–93) was a layman, a physician and antiquary, who lived in rural Brecknockshire in the Usk valley. Christians are so used to saying that religion is not just for Sunday, that it is a pleasant change to celebrate it as Vaughan does here as a taste of heaven on earth.

Sundays

> Bright shadows of true Rest! some shoots of blisse,
>   Heaven once a week;
> The next world's gladnes prepossest in this;
>   A day to seek
> Eternity in time; the steps by which
> We Climb above all ages; Lamps that light

Man through his heap of dark days; and the rich,
And full redemption of the whole week's flight.

The Pulleys unto headlong man; time's bower;
   The narrow way;
Transplanted Paradise; God's walking houre;
   The Cool o'th' day;
The Creature's Jubilee; God's parle with dust;
Heaven here; Man on those hills of Myrrh, and flowres;
Angels descending; the Returns of Trust;
A Gleam of glory, after six-days-showres.

The Churches' love-feasts; Time's Prerogative,
   And Interest
Deducted from the whole; The Combs, and hive,
   And home of rest.
The milky way Chalkt out with Suns; a Clue
That guides through erring hours; and in full story
A taste of Heav'n on earth; the pledge, and Cue
Of a full feast; And the Out Courts of glory.

Envoi
Hilaire Belloc

Hilaire Belloc (1870–1953) had the ability, it has been observed, to slip from the solemn to the humorous, and from the satirical to the sublime. Here he begins satirically, taking as his subject a newspaper report of one of those forgotten Victorian wrangles about the permissibility under English law of placing images in churches. The refrain 'A Female Figure with a Child' takes on a moving power in the Envoi.

Ballade of Illegal Ornaments

'... the controversy was ended by His Lordship, who wrote to the Incumbent ordering him to remove from the Church all Illegal Ornaments at once, and especially a Female Figure with a Child.'

When that the Eternal deigned to look
On us poor folk to make us free,
He chose a Maiden, whom He took
From Nazareth in Galilee;
Since when the Islands of the Sea,
The Field, the City, and the Wild
Proclaim aloud triumphantly
A Female Figure with a Child.

These Mysteries profoundly shook
The Reverend Doctor Leigh, D.D.,
Who therefore stuck into a Nook
(Or Niche) of his Incumbency
An Image filled with majesty
To represent the Undefiled,
The Universal Mother – She –
A Female Figure with a Child.

His Bishop, having read a book
Which proved as plain as plain could be
That all the Mutts had been mistook
Who talked about a Trinity,
Wrote off at once to Doctor Leigh
In manner very far from mild,
And said: 'Remove them instantly!
A Female Figure with a Child!'

Envoi
Prince Jesus, in mine Agony,
Permit me, broken and defiled,
Through blurred and glazing eyes to see
A Female Figure with a Child.

Sources and further reading

p. 1: Francis Kilvert's diaries were edited, though not in full, by William Plomer in three volumes (London: Jonathan Cape, 1938–40). There is an abridged paperback in print (London: Ebury Press, 1999).

p. 3: Robert Herrick. From *The Poetical Works* edited by F.W. Moorman (Oxford: Oxford University Press, 1915). Selections are in print in various paperback editions.

p. 4: Walter Hilton. From *The Scale of Perfection* edited by Dom Gerard Sitwell OSB (London, Burns and Oates, 1953). Under the title *The Ladder of Perfection* it is available as a Penguin paperback (Harmondsworth: Penguin, 1957).

p. 7: John Bunyan. *The Pilgrim's Progress* is in print in paperback. George Offor's big three-volume edition of Bunyan's *Works* (London, 1862) is useful. Oxford University Press has been issuing expensive volumes of a learned edition. *The Poems*, edited by Graham Midgeley, were published as one volume (Oxford, 1980).

p. 9: William Cowper. From *The Poetical Works of William Cowper*, edited by Henry Frowde (London: Oxford University Press, 1911). Selected poems are available in paperback. A selection of Cowper's letters tracing his life is published by Carcanet. A print-on-demand full edition of the prose and letters is published in five volumes by Oxford University Press at an astonishingly high price.

p. 13: Christina Rossetti. From *Seek and Find* (London, 1879). Her poems are in print from several paperback publishers. Four volumes of her religious prose works (*Called to be Saints*: *The Minor Festivals Devotionally Studied*; *Letter and Spirit*: *Notes on the Commandments*; *Time*

*Flie*s: *A Reading Diary*; and *The Face of the Deep*: *A Devotional Commentary on The Apocalypse*) have been edited by Maria Keaton (Chicago: Thoemmes Continuum, 2003). *Selected Prose of Christina Rossetti* was edited by David A. Kent and P.G. Stanwood (London: Macmillan, 1998).

p. 15: Nehemiah Grew. From *Cosmologia Sacra or a Discourse of the Universe as it is the Creature and Kingdom of God* (London: 1701).

p. 18: Marbod. From *More Latin Lyrics* translated by Helen Waddell, edited by Dame Felicitas Corrigan (London: Gollancz, 1976).

p. 19: Lizette Woodworth Reese. Her *Selected Poems* (New York: George H. Doran, 1926) can be found cheaply second-hand.

p. 20: William Habington. His *Poems* were edited by Kenneth Allott (London: Hodder and Stoughton, 1948).

p. 21: Augustine. *The Sermons* are translated in 11 volumes by Edmund Hill OP (Hyde Park, NY: New City Press, 1990 onwards). Of Augustine's *Confessions*, modern translations include those of Henry Chadwick (Oxford Paperback, 1998) and F.J. Sheed (London: Continuum, Sheed and Ward, 1987). Frederick Van Der Meer's *Augustine the Bishop* gives a vivid picture of him in his time and place, and an up-to-date treatment from a classical historian is Serge Lancel's *St Augustine* (translated by Antonia M. Nevill, London: SCM Press, 2002).

p. 22: Bede. From *The Biographical Writings*, translated by J.A. Giles (London: Bohn, 1845). *The Life of Cuthbert* is included in *The Age of Bede*, edited by D.H. Farmer (Harmondsworth: Penguin 1998).

p. 23: Gerard Manley Hopkins. The poems and excerpts from the journals and letters are available in paperback (*The Major Works*, Oxford: Oxford University Press, 2002).

p. 24: Robert Herrick. See note for page 3.

p. 26: Alcuin. From *More Latin Lyrics* translated by Helen Waddell, edited by Dame Felicitas Corrigan (London: Victor Gollancz, 1976). The standard Latin text of Alcuin's poetry is in *Poetae Latini Aevi Carolini*, edited by Ernst Dummler (Berlin, 1881). For his life and times see *Alcuin, Friend of Charlemagne, his World and Work*, by E. Duckett (1965). An excellent introduction to Alcuin's influence on the worship of the Church year is Gerald Ellard's *Master Alcuin, Liturgist* (Chicago: Loyola University Press, 1956).

p. 26: John Gother. From *The Spiritual Works of the Rev John Gother*, Vol I (Newcastle, 1792).

p. 29: Charles Wesley. *Charles Wesley: A Reader* (Oxford: Oxford University Press, 2000) contains selected hymns, poems, sermons and letters.

p. 30: Aelred. From *Spiritual Friendship*, translated by Mary Eugenia Laker (Kalamazoo, MI: Cistercian Publications, 1977).

p. 32: Jeremy Taylor. From *The Whole Works of the Right Rev Jeremy Taylor DD*, Vol. VIII (London, 1883).

p. 33: Francis de Sales. From *The Library of St Francis de Sales*, translated by Henry Benedict Mackey, Vol. I (London: Burns and Oates, 1901). A modern selection of letters to and from St Jeanne de Chantal is entitled *Letters of Spiritual Direction* (New York: Paulist Press, 1988).

p. 34: John Clare. From *Poems of John Clare's Madness*, edited by Geoffrey Grigson (London: Routledge and Kegan Paul, 1949). There is an excellent biography by Jonathan Bate (London: Picador, 2003), who has also selected a volume of Clare's poetry, *I Am* (New York: Farrar, Straus and Giroux, 2003).

p. 35: Anne Bradstreet. The standard edition is *The Works of Anne Bradstreet*, edited by Jeannine Hensley (Cambridge, MA: Harvard University Press, 1967).

p. 37: G.K. Chesterton. From his *Autobiography* (London: Hutchinson, 1936). A good anthology is *The Essential G.K. Chesterton*, edited by P.J. Kavanagh (Oxford: Oxford University Press, 1987). Chesterton's earlier apologia, *Orthodoxy*, and the book that came before it, *Heretics*, are published together in a neat hardback (Nashville, TN: Nelson Reference, 2000). As an e-book, *Orthodoxy* can be downloaded from amazon.com for a low fee, as can his extraordinary novel *The Man Who Was Thursday*, which is also in paperback (Harmondsworth: Penguin, 1990).

p. 40: John Clare. See note for page 34.

p. 40: Julian of Norwich. Adapted from *Revelations of Divine Love*, edited by Grace Warrack (London: Methuen, 1901) That translation is full of tiresome archaisms. There is a translation in Penguin Classics, but there the reader sometimes wonders exactly what the orginal wording was (for Julian uses some daring phraseology). An edition in Middle English is published by the Early English Text Sociey (Woodbridge: Boydell & Brewer).

p. 43: John Henry Newman. From *Parochial and Plain Sermons*, Vol V (London: Rivingtons, 1882). Newman's books, particularly the *Apologia* and *The Development of Christian Doctrine*, can be found second-hand. There is an excellent biography by Ian Ker (Oxford: Clarendon Press, 1989), who has also edited *Selected Sermons* (New York: Paulist Press, 1994).

p. 49: Mother Teresa of Calcutta. A selection of her prayers and teaching may be found in the inexpensive paperback *A Fruitful Branch on the Vine, Jesus* (Cincinnati, OH: St Anthony Messenger Press, 2000).

p. 50: John Tillotson. From *The Works of the Most Reverend Dr John Tillotson* (London, 1793).

p. 52: Sydney Smith. From *The Letters of Sydney Smith*, edited by Nowell C. Smith (Oxford: Clarendon Press, 1953).

p. 53: Frederick William Faber. From *Notes on Doctrinal and Spiritual Subjects*, Vol. II (London: Burns and Oates, 1866). There is a biography by Ronald Chapman (London: Burns and Oates, 1961).

p. 55: Oscar Wilde. *De Profundis* is in print in paperback, most cheaply from Dover Publications (Mineola, NY: 1997).

p. 57: George Herbert. *The Complete English Works* are available in economical hardback from Everyman's Library (London: 1995).

p. 59: Gerard Manley Hopkins. See note for page 23.

p. 59: William Law. From *A Serious Call to a Devout and Holy Life* (London: Methuen, 1899). It can be found in paperback or cheaply as a second-hand hardback.

p. 64: George MacDonald. From *Unspoken Sermons*, Vol. I (London: Alexander Strahan, 1867). These have been reprinted by Johannesen Printing and Publishing, which has published 48 works by MacDonald in 44 volumes and made many available on the internet at www.johannesen.com

p. 72: Bede. From *On Tobit* and the *Canticle of Habakkuk*, edited by Sean Connolly (Dublin: Four Courts Press, 1997).

p. 74: Ronald Knox. From *St Paul's Gospel* (London: Sheed and Ward, 1950). Knox's translation of the Bible is easy to find second-hand. So is *Enthusiasm*, in a well-produced hardback edition. It has been republished in paperback. Evelyn Waugh wrote a memoir, *Ronald Knox*, which has a gloomy air.

p. 80: John Morris. From *The Last Illness of His Eminence Cardinal Wiseman* (London: Burns, Lambert and Oates, 1865).

p. 83: Thomas of Celano. From *Saint Francis of Assisi: Omnibus of Sources*, 2 vols (Quincy, IL: Franciscan Press, Quincy University, 1991).

p. 87: Edward Bouverie Pusey. From *Parochial Sermons by the Rev E.B. Pusey*, Vol. I (Oxford: Parker, 1864).

p. 89: Alcuin. See note for page 26.

p. 89: C.S. Lewis. From *A Grief Observed* (London: Faber, 1961).

p. 92: Samuel Johnson. The standard edition is from Yale. *Diaries, Prayers and Annals*, edited by E.L. McAdam make up Vol. I (New Haven, CT: Yale University Press, 1958).

p. 93: P.J. Kavanagh. From *Selected Poems* (London: Chatto and Windus, 1982). His *Poems* are published by Carcanet (Manchester, 2003), as are *A Kind of Journal* (collected columns, 2003) and his classic memoir *The Perfect Stranger*.

p. 94: Hilaire Belloc. From *Sonnets and Verse* (London: Duckworth, 1945). *The Path to Rome*, the account of his long walk, has been republished by Ignatius Press (Fort Collins, CO: 2003).

p. 95: Dorothy L. Sayers. *The Poetry of Dorothy L. Sayers*, edited by Ralph Hone (London: Dorothy L. Sayers Society, 1996).

p. 96: John Clare. See note for page 34.

p. 97: Psalm 38. Apart from the Prayer Book version and the King James version, the psalms have been arranged for singing to the psalmody of Joseph Gelineau (the Grail version – London: Collins, 1966), although this text has more recently been disrupted by adjustments to make the language inclusive. The Latin Vulgate and King James texts may be found on the internet. *The Authorised Daily Prayer Book of the United Hebrew Congregations of the British Commonwealth*, with Hebrew and English text translated by the Revd S. Singer (London: Eyre and Spottiswoode, 1962) can be found second-hand.

p. 98: John Fisher. From *The English Works of John Fisher* (London: Early English Text Society, 1876, reprinted 1999, distributed by Boydell and Brewer, Woobridge, Suffolk). There is a biography by Maria Dowling: *Fisher of Men* (Basingstoke: Palgrave Macmillan, 1999).

p. 100: The best way to buy a missal is either by visiting a good bookshop (such as St Pauls by Westminster Cathedral, London SW1, if you live in London) or on the internet. The internet also provides Latin and English versions of the Easter liturgy.

p. 102: Edward Taylor. The standard edition is *The Poems of Edward Taylor*, edited by Donald E. Stanford (New Haven, CT: Yale University Press, 1960).

p. 107: Rorate Coeli. Solesmes, the monastery that re-established reliable texts and chants, included this Advent prayer in its *Manual of Gregorian Chant* (Rome-Tournai: 1903). A compact disc including the Rorate – *Chants Populaires de la Liturgie Latine* by the choir of Solesmes – is published by the Abbaye Saint-Pierre, 72300 Solesmes, France. It has a website.

p. 110: George Herbert. See note for page 57.

p. 112: Thomas More. The version of the *Dialogue of Comfort against Tribulation* used here is from the edition published by Sheed and

Ward (London: 1951) adapted from the earlier Everyman edition. An expensive old-spelling version is published by Yale University Press (New Haven, CT and London, 1976).

p. 117: John Clare. See note for page 34.

p. 118: Christopher Smart. From *Jubilate Agno*, edited by W.H. Bond (London: Rupert Hart-Davis, 1954)

p. 124: Augustine. An up-to-date translation of *The Trinity* is by Edmund Hill OP in Part I, Vol. 5 of *The Works of St Augustine* (Brooklyn, NY: New City Press, 1991)

p. 129: Prudentius. From *More Latin Lyrics* translated by Helen Waddell, edited by Dame Felicitas Corrigan (London: Gollancz, 1976). Parallel Latin and English appear in the two-volume Loeb collection (Cambridge, MA: Harvard University Press, 1949). A translation of the poems was published by The Catholic University of America (Washington DC, 1965).

p. 130: Richard Baxter. From *The Saints' Everlasting Rest* (London: 1811). A current edition is published by Christian Focus Publications (Fearn, Tain, Ross-shire: 2000)

p. 133: John Mabbe. From *Devout Contemplations* (London: Adam Islip, 1629)

p. 134: William Habington: His *Poems* were edited by Kenneth Allott (London: Hodder and Stoughton, 1948)

p. 135: Augustine Baker. From *Holy Wisdom, Extracted out of more than Forty Treatises and Methodically Digested by Serenus Cressy* (1657), edited by Abbot Sweeney (London: Burns and Oates, 1911). This was republished in the Orchard Series (Burns and Oates), and again by A. Clarke Books in 1972.

p. 138: Emily Dickinson. The history of the editions of Emily Dickinson's poems is a mess. A text based on surviving manuscripts makes up *The Complete Poems*, edited by Thomas H. Johnson (London: Faber, 1970).

p. 139: Boethius. Metrum 6 from Book 4 of the *Consolatione Philosophiae*; translation from *The Works of Henry Vaughan*, edited by Leonard Cyril Martin (Oxford: Oxford University Press, 1914).

p. 142: John Spencer. From *Things New and Old* (London: 1658). A new edition was published in two volumes by William Tegg in London, 1869.

p. 143: Thomas Traherne. *Centuries, Poems and Thanksgivings* was edited by H.M. Margoliouth (Oxford: Oxford University Press, 1958). Various selections are to be found in paperback.

p. 148: Ambrose. From *More Latin Lyrics* translated by Helen Waddell, edited by Dame Felicitas Corrigan (London: Gollancz, 1976).

p. 149: G.K. Chesterton. From *The Collected Poems* (London: Methuen, 1933).

p. 157: Bede. From *More Latin Lyrics* translated by Helen Waddell, edited by Dame Felicitas Corrigan (London: Gollancz, 1976).

p. 158: Thomas à Kempis. From *The Christian's Pattern*, translated by John Wesley (London: 1815).

p. 160: Francs Kilvert. See note for page 1.

p. 161: Richard of Chichester. *Saint Richard of Chichester: the Sources for his Life* was edited by David Jones (Lewes: Sussex Record Society, 1995).

p. 161: Francis de Sales. From *A Treatise of the Love of God*, translated into English by Miles Car, Priest of the English Colledge of Doway (Douay: Gerard Pinchon, 1630). Both *The Love of God* and *An Introduction to the Devout Life* were published in the Orchard series by Burns and Oates, and these are easily come by second-hand.

p. 166: Anonymous. Found on a card in a prayer book.

p. 167: John Donne. The poetry is in print. Evelyn Simpson's selection of 10 sermons has been republished as *John Donne's Sermons on the Psalms and Gospels* (Berkeley, CA: University of California Press, 2003). Extracts from sermons are in *John Donne: Selected Prose*, edited by Helen Gardiner and T. Healy (Oxford 1967). There is an expensive learned edition of the sermons in 10 volumes (Berkeley, CA: University of California, 1953–61).

p. 175: Lancelot Andrewes. From *Ninety-Six Sermons*, Vol. III (Oxford: Parker, 1841). A small volume, *Selected Writings*, edited by P.E. Hewison, is published by Fyfield Books (Manchester: Carcanet, 1995).

p. 179: Harry Williams. From *The Joy of God* (London: Continuum, 2002).

p. 184: Hugh of St Victor. From *Selected Spiritual Writings* (London: Faber, 1962).

p. 185: John Spencer. See note for page 142.

p. 186: John Wesley. From *The Works of the Rev John Wesley* (London: Wesleyan Methodist Bookroom, 1872). There is a good introductory biography, *John Wesley, a Personal Portrait* by Ralph Waller (London: SPCK, 2003).

p. 187: Philip Doddridge. From *The Family Expositor* (London: 1739–56).

p. 189: Mark Allen and Ruth Burrows. From *Letters on Prayer* (London: Sheed and Ward, 1999). Among Ruth Burrows' books are *Ascent to Love: The Spiritual Teaching of St John of the Cross* (London: Sheed and Ward, 2000) and *Before the Living God* (London: Sheed and Ward, 1979). Mark Allen has also written a book for parents, *First Holy Communion* (Burns and Oates, 1999).

p. 195: John Donne. See note for page 167.

p. 195: Thomas à Kempis. From *The Imitation of Christ, Now for the First Time Set Forth in Rhythmic Sentences*, published anonymously with a preface by H.P. Liddon (London: Elliot Stock, 1889). There is a choice of various modern paperback editions.

p. 199: John Spencer. See note for page 142.

p. 200: Lucy Herbert. From *The Devotions of the Lady Lucy Herbert of Powis*, edited by John Morris SJ (London: Burns and Oates, 1873).

p. 202: Henry Vaughan. From *The Works of Henry Vaughan*, edited by Leonard Cyril Martin (Oxford: Oxford University Press, 1914).

p. 203: Hilaire Belloc. From *Sonnets and Verse* (London: Duckworth, 1945).